I0022566

Lord Bacon

Pagan Mythology

Or, The Wisdom of the Ancients

Lord Bacon

Pagan Mythology
Or, The Wisdom of the Ancients

ISBN/EAN: 9783337179649

Printed in Europe, USA, Canada, Australia, Japan

Cover: Foto ©ninafisch / pixelio.de

More available books at **www.hansebooks.com**

PAGAN MYTHOLOGY

OR THE

WISDOM OF THE ANCIENTS

BY

LORD BACON.

LONDON:

PROGRESSIVE PUBLISHING COMPANY,

28 STONECUTTER STREET, E.C.

1891.

LONDON :

PRINTED AND PUBLISHED BY G. W. FOOTE,

28 STONECUTTER STREET, E.C.

Pagan Mythology

OR

THE WISDOM OF THE ANCIENTS.

PREFACE.

THE earliest antiquity lies buried in silence and oblivion, excepting the remains we have of it in sacred writ. This silence was succeeded by poetical fables, and these, at length, by the writings we now enjoy ; so that the concealed and secret learning of the ancients seems separated from the history and knowledge of the following ages by a veil, or partition wall of fables, interposing between the things that are lost and those that remain.

Many may imagine that I am here entering upon a work of fancy, or amusement, and design to use a poetical liberty, in explaining poetical fables. It is true, fables in general are composed of ductile matter, that may be drawn into great variety by a witty talent or an inventive genius, and be delivered of plausible meanings which they never contained. But this procedure has already been carried to excess ; and great numbers, to procure the sanction of antiquity to their own notions and inventions, have miserably wrested and abused the fables of the ancients.

Nor is this only a late or unfrequent practice, but of ancient date, and common even to this day. Thus Chrysippus, like an interpreter of dreams, attributed

the opinions of the Stoics to the poets of old ; and the
chemists, at present, more childishly apply the poetical
transformations to their experiments of the furnace.
And though I have well weighed and considered all
this, and thoroughly seen into the levity which the
mind indulges for allegories and allusions, yet I cannot
but retain a high value for the ancient mythology.
And, certainly, it were very injudicious to suffer the
fondness and licentiousness of a few to detract from
the honor of allegory and parable in general. This
would be rash, and almost profane ; for, since religion
delights in such shadows and disguises, to abolish them
were, in a manner, to prohibit all intercourse betwixt
things divine and human.

Upon deliberate consideration, my judgment is, that
a concealed instruction and allegory was originally
intended in many of the ancient fables. This opinion
may, in some respect, be owing to the veneration I
have for antiquity, but more to observing that some
fables discover a great and evident similitude, relation,
and connection with the thing they signify, as well in
the structure of the fable as in the propriety of the
names whereby the persons or actors are characterised ;
insomuch, that no one could positively deny a sense
and meaning to be from the first intended, and purposely shadowed out in them. For who can hear that
Fame, after the giants were destroyed, sprung up as
their posthumous sister, and not apply it to the clamor
of parties and the seditious rumors which commonly
fly about for a time upon the quelling of insurrections ?
Or who can read how the giant Typhon cut out and
carried away Jupiter's sinews—which Mercury afterwards stole and again restored to Jupiter—and not
presently observe that this allegory denotes strong and
powerful rebellions, which cut away from kings their
sinews, both of money and authority ; and that the

way to have them restored is by lenity, affability, and
prudent edicts, which soon reconcile, and as it were
steal upon the affections of the subject ? Or who, upon
hearing that memorable expedition of the gods against
the giants, when the braying of Silenus's ass greatly
contributed in putting the giants to flight, does not
clearly conceive that this directly points at the monstrous enterprises of rebellious subjects, which are
frequently frustrated and disappointed by vain fears
and empty rumors?

Again, the conformity and purport of the names is
frequently manifest and self-evident. Thus Metis,
the wife of Jupiter, plainly signifies counsel ; Typhon,
swelling; Pan, universality ; Nemesis, revenge ; etc.
Nor is it a wonder, if sometimes a piece of history or
other things are introduced, by way of ornament ; or
if the times of the action are confounded ; or if part
of one fable be tacked to another ; or if the allegory
be new turned ; for all this must necessarily happen,
as the fables were the inventions of men who lived in
different ages and had different views ; some of them
being ancient, others more modern ; some having an
eye to natural philosophy, and others to morality or
civil policy.

It may pass for a farther indication of a concealed
and secret meaning, that some of these fables are so
absurd and idle in their narration as to show and pro-
claim an allegory, even afar off. A fable that carries
probability with it may be supposed invented for
pleasure, or in imitation of history ; but those that
could never be conceived or related in this way must
surely have a different use. For example, what a
monstrous fiction is this, that Jupiter should take Metis
to wife, and as soon as he found her pregnant eat her
up, whereby he also conceived, and out of his head
brought forth Pallas armed. Certainly no mortal could,

but for the sake of the moral it couches, invent such
an absurd dream as this, so much out of the road of
thought !

But the argument of most weight with me is this,
that many of these fables by no means appear to have
been invented by the persons who relate and divulge
them, whether Homer, Hesiod, or others ; for if I
were assured they first flowed from those later times
and authors that transmit them to us, I should never
expect anything singularly great or noble from such
an origin. But whoever attentively considers the
thing will find that these fables are delivered down
and related by those writers, not as matters then first
invented and proposed, but as things received and
embraced in earlier ages. Besides, as they are dif-
erently related by writers nearly of the same ages, it
is easily perceived that the relators drew from the
common stock of ancient tradition, and varied but in
point of embellishment, which is their own. And
this principally raises my esteem of these fables,
which I receive, not as the product of the age, or
invention of the poets, but as sacred relics, gentle
whispers, and the breath of better times, that from the
traditions of more ancient nations came, at length, into
the flutes and trumpets of the Greeks. But if any one
shall, notwithstanding this, contend that allegories are
always adventitious, or imposed upon the ancient
fables, and no way native or genuinely contained in
them, we might here leave him undisturbed in that
gravity of judgment he affects (though we cannot help
accounting it something dull and phlegmatic), and if it
were worth the trouble, proceed to another kind of
argument.

Men have proposed to answer two different and
contrary ends by the use of parable ; for parables serve
as well to instruct or illustrate as to wrap up or envelop,

so that though, for the present, we drop the concealed use, and suppose the ancient fables to be vague, un-determinate things, formed for amusement, still the other use must remain, and can never be given up. And every man, of any learning, must readily allow that this method of instructing is grave, sober, or exceedingly useful, and sometimes necessary in the sciences, as it opens an easy and familiar passage to the human understanding, in all new discoveries that are abstruse and out of the road of vulgar opinions. Hence, in the first ages, when such inventions and con-clusions of the human reason as are now trite and common were new and little known, all things abounded with fables, parables, similes, comparisons, and allusions, which were not intended to conceal, but to inform and teach, whilst the minds of men con-tinued rude and unpractised in matters of subtility and speculation, or even impatient, and in a manner uncapable of receiving such things as did not directly fall under and strike the senses. For as hieroglyphics were in use before writing, so were parables in use before arguments. And even to this day, if any man would let new light in upon the human understanding, and conquer prejudice, without raising contests, animosities, opposition, or disturbance, he must still go in the same path, and have recourse to the like method of allegory, metaphor, and allusion.

To conclude, the knowledge of the early ages was either great or happy ; great, if they by design made this use of trope and figure : happy, if, whilst they had other views, they afforded matter and occasion to such noble contemplations. Let either be the case, our pains, perhaps, will not be misemployed, whether we illustrate antiquity or things themselves.

The like indeed has been attempted by others ; but to speak ‚ingenuously, their great and voluminous labors have almost destroyed the energy, the efficacy, and grace of the thing, whilst, being unskilled in nature, and their learning no more than that of common-place, they have applied the sense of the parables to certain general and vulgar matters, without reaching to their real purport, genuine interpretation, and full depth. For myself, therefore, I expect to appear new in these common things, because, leaving untouched such as are sufficiently plain and open, I shall drive only at those that are either deep or rich.

I.—CASSANDRA, OR DIVINATION.

EXPLAINED OF TOO FREE AND UNSEASONABLE ADVICE.

The Poets relate that Apollo, falling in love with Cassandra, was still deluded and put off by her, yet fed with hopes, till she had got from him the gift of prophecy ; and having now obtained her end, she flatly rejected his suit. Apollo, unable to recall his rash gift, yet enraged to be outwitted by a girl, annexed this penalty to it, that though she should always prophesy true, she should never be believed ; whence her divinations were always slighted, even when she again and again predicted the ruin of her country.

Explanation.—This fable seems invented to express the insignificance of unreasonable advice. For they who are conceited, stubborn, or intractable, and listen not to the instructions of Apollo, the god of harmony, so as to learn and observe the modulations and measures of affairs, the sharps and flats of discourse, the difference between judicious and vulgar ears, and the proper times of speech and silence, let them be ever so intelligent, and ever so frank of their advice, or their counsels ever so good and just, yet all their endeavors, either of persuasion or force, are of little significance, and rather hasten the ruin of those they advise. But, at last, when the calamitous event has made the sufferers feel the effect of their neglect, they too late reverence their advisers, as deep, foreseeing, and faithful prophets.

Of this we have a remarkable instance in Cato of Utica, who discovered afar off, and long foretold, the approaching ruin of his country, both in the first conspiracy, and as it was prosecuted in the civil war between Cæsar and Pompey yet did no good the while, but rather hurt the commonwealth, and hurried on its destruction, which Cicero wisely observed in these words : "Cato, indeed, judges excellently, but prejudices the state ; for he speaks as in the commonwealth of Plato, and not as in the dregs of Romulus."

II.—TYPHON : OR A REBEL.

EXPLAINED OF REBELLION.

The fable runs, that Juno, enraged at Jupiter's bringing forth Pallas without her assistance, incessantly solicited all the gods and goddesses. that she might produce without Jupiter : and having by violence and importunity obtained the grant, she struck the earth, and thence immediately sprung up Typhon, a huge and dreadful monster, whom she committed to the nursing of a serpent. As soon as he was grown up, this monster waged war on Jupiter, and taking him prisoner in the battle, carried him away on his shoulders, into a remote and obscure quarter : and there cutting out the sinews of his hands and feet, he bore them off, leaving Jupiter behind miserably maimed and mangled.

But Mercury afterwards stole these sinews from Typhon and restored them to Jupiter. Hence, recovering his strength, Jupiter again pursues the monster; first wounds him with a stroke of his thunder, when serpents arose from the blood of the wound : and now the monster being dismayed, and taking to flight, Jupiter next darted Mount Ætna upon him, and crushed him with the weight.

Explanation.—This fable seems designed to express the various fates of kings, and the turns that rebellions sometimes take, in kingdoms. For princes may be justly esteemed married to their states, as Jupiter to Juno ; but it sometimes happens, that, being depraved by long wielding of the sceptre, and growing tyrannical, they would engross all to themselves ; and slighting the counsel of their senators and nobles, conceive by themselves ; that is, govern according to their own arbitrary will and pleasure. This inflames the people, and makes them endeavor to create and set up some head of their own. Such designs are generally set on foot by the secret motion and instigation of the peers and nobles, under whose connivance the common sort are prepared for rising : whence proceeds a swell in the state, which is appositely denoted by the nursing of Typhon. This growing posture of affairs is fed by the natural depravity, and malignant dispositions of the vulgar, which to kings is an envenomed serpent. And now the disaffected, uniting their force, at length break out into open rebellion, which, producing infinite mischiefs, both to prince and people, is represented by the horrid and multiplied deformity of Typhon, with his hundred heads, denoting the divided powers ; his flaming mouths, denoting fire and devastation ; his girdles of snakes, denoting sieges and destruction ; his iron hands, slaughter and cruelty ; his eagle's talons, rapine and plunder ; his plumed body, perpetual rumors, contradictory accounts, etc. And sometimes these rebellions grow so high, that kings are obliged, as if carried on the backs of the rebels, to quit tho throne, and retire to some remote and obscure part of their dominions, with the loss of their sinews, both of money and majesty,

But if now they prudently bear this reverse of fortune, they may, in a short time, by the assistance of Mercury, recover their sinews again; that is, by becoming moderate and affable ; reconciling the minds and affections of the people to them, by gracious speeches and prudent proclamations, which will win over the subject cheerfully to afford new aids and supplies, and add fresh vigor to authority. But prudent and wary princes here seldom incline to try fortune by a war, yet do their utmost, by some grand exploit, to crush the reputation of the rebels : and if the attempt succeeds, the rebels, conscious of the wound received, and distrustful of their cause, first betake themselves to broken and empty threats, like the hissings of serpents ; and next, when matters are grown desperate, to flight. And now, when they thus begin to shrink, it is safe and seasonable for kings to pursue them with their forces, and the whole strength of the kingdom ; thus effectually quashing and suppressing them, as it were by the weight of a mountain.

III.—THE CYCLOPS : OR THE MINISTERS OF TERROR.

EXPLAINED OF BASE COURT OFFICERS.

It is related that the Cyclops, for their savageness and cruelty, were by Jupiter first thrown into Tartarus, and there condemned to perpetual imprisonment ; but, that afterwards, Tellus, persuaded Jupiter it would be for his service to release them, and employ them in forging thunderbolts. This he accordingly did ; and they, with unwearied pains and diligence, hammered out his bolts, and other instruments of terror, with a frightful and continual din of the anvil.

It happened long after, that Jupiter was displeased with Æsculapius, the son of Apollo, for having, by the art of medicine, restored a dead man to life ; but concealing his indignation, because the action in itself was pious and illustrious, he secretly incensed the Cyclops against him, who, without remorse, presently slew him with their thunderbolts : in revenge whereof, Apollo, with Jupiter's connivance, shot them all dead with his arrows.

Explanation.—This fable seems to point at the behavior of princes, who, having cruel, bloody, and oppressive ministers, first punish and displace them ; but afterwards, by the advice of Tellus, that is, some earthly-minded and ignoble person, employ them again, to serve a turn, when there is occasion for cruelty in execution, or severity in exaction : but these ministers being base in their nature, whet by their former disgrace, and well aware of what is expected from them, use double diligence in their office ; till, proceeding unwarily, and over-eager to gain favor, they sometimes, from the private nods and ambiguous orders of their prince, perform some odious or execrable action : When princes, to decline the envy themselves, and knowing they shall never want such tools at their back, drop them, and give them up to the friends and followers of the injured person ; thus exposing them, as sacrifices to revenge and popular odium : whence with great applause, acclamations, and good wishes to the prince, these miscreants at last meet with their desert.

IV.—NARCISSUS : OR SELF-LOVE.

Narcissus is said to have been extremely beautiful and comely, but intolerably proud and disdainful ; so that, pleased with himself, and scorning the world, he led a solitary life in the woods ; hunting only with a few followers, who were his professed admirers, amongst whom the nymph Echo was his constant attendant. In this method of life it was once his fate to approach a clear fountain, where he laid himself down to rest, in the noonday heat ; when, beholding his image in the water, he fell into such a rapture and admiration of himself, that he could by no means be got away, but remained continually fixed and gazing, till at length he was turned into a flower, of his own name, which appears early in the spring, and is consecrated to the infernal deities, Pluto, Proserpine, and the Furies.

Explanation.—This fable seems to paint the behavior and fortune of those who, for their beauty, or other endowments, wherewith nature (without any industry of their own) has graced and adorned them, are extravagantly fond of themselves : for men of such a disposition generally affect retirement, and absence from public affairs ; as a life of business must necessarily subject them to many neglects and contempts, which might disturb and ruffle their minds : whence such persons commonly lead a solitary, private, and shadowy life ; see little company, and those only such as highly admire and reverence them ; or, like an echo, assent to all they say.

And they who are depraved, and rendered still fonder of themselves by this custom, grow strangely indolent, unactive, and perfectly stupid. The Narcissus, a spring flower, is an elegant emblem of this temper, which at first flourishes, and is talked of, but when ripe, frustrates the expectation conceived of it.

And that this flower should be sacred to the infernal powers, carries out the allusion still farther ; because men of this humor are perfectly useless in all respects ; for whatever yields no fruit, but passes, and is no more, like the way of a ship in the sea, was by the ancients consecrated to the infernal shades and powers.

V.—THE RIVER STYX: OR LEAGUES.

EXPLAINED OF NECESSITY, IN THE OATHS OR SOLEMN
LEAGUES OF PRINCES.

The only solemn oath, by which the gods irrevocably obliged themselves, is a well-known thing, and makes a part of many ancient fables. To this oath they did not invoke any celestial divinity, or divine attribute, but only called to witness the river Styx ; which, with many meanders, surrounds the infernal court of Dis. For this form alone, and none but this, was held inviolable and obligatory : and the punishment of falsifying it, was that dreaded one of being excluded, for a certain number of years, the table of the gods.

Explanation.—This fable seems invented to show the nature of the compacts and confederacies of princes ; which, though ever so solemnly and religiously sworn to, prove but little the more binding for it : so that oaths in this case seem used, rather for decorum, reputation, and ceremony, than for fidelity, security, and effectuating. And though these oaths were strengthened with the bonds of affinity, which are the links and ties of nature, and again, by mutual services and good offices, yet we see all this will generally give way to ambition, convenience, and the thirst of power ; the rather, because it is easy for princes, under various specious pretences, to defend, disguise, and conceal their ambitious desires and insincerity ; having no judge to call them to account. There is, however, one true and proper confirmation of their faith, though no celestial divinity ; but that great divinity of princes, Necessity ; or, the danger of the state ; and the securing of advantage.

This necessity is elegantly represented by Styx, the fatal river, that can never be crossed back. And this deity it was, which Iphicrates the Athenian invoked in making a league : and because he roundly and openly avows what most others studiously conceal, it may be proper to give his own words. Observing that the Lacedæmonians were inventing and proposing a variety of securities, sanctions, and bonds of alliance, he interrupted them thus : " There may, indeed, my friends, be one bond and means of security between us ; and that is, for you to demonstrate you have delivered into our hands such things as that if you had the greatest desire to hurt us you could not be able." Therefore, if the power of offending be taken away, or if by a breach of compact there be danger of destruction or diminution to the state or tribute, then it is that covenants will be ratified, and confirmed, as it were, by the Stygian oath, whilst there remains an impending danger of being prohibited and excluded the banquet of the gods ; by which expression the ancients denoted the rights and prerogatives, the the affluence and the felicities, of empire and dominion.

VI.—PAN : OR NATURE.

EXPLAINED OF NATURAL PHILOSOPHY.

The ancients have, with great exactness, delineated universal nature under the person of Pan. They leave

his origin doubtful ; some asserting him the son of
Mercury, and others the common offspring of all
Penelope's suitors. The latter supposition doubtless
occasioned some later rivals to entitle this ancient
fable Penelope ; a thing frequently practised when the
earlier relations are applied to more modern characters
and persons, though sometimes with great absurdity
and ignorance, as in the present case ; for Pan was one
of the ancientest gods, and long before the time of
Ulysses; besides, Penelope was venerated by antiquity
for her matronal chastity. A third sort will have him
the issue of Jupiter and Hybris, that is, Reproach.
But whatever his origin was, the Destinies are allowed
his sisters.

He is described by antiquity, with pyramidal horns
reaching up to heaven, a rough and shaggy body, a
very long beard, of a biform figure, human above, half
brute below, ending in goat's feet. His arms, or
ensigns of power, are, a pipe in his left hand, composed
of seven reeds; in his right a crook; and he wore for
his mantle a leopard's skin.

His attributes and titles were the god of hunters,
shepherds, and all the rural inhabitants ; president of
the mountains ; and, after Mercury, the next messenger
of the gods. He was also held the leader and ruler of
the Nymphs, who continually danced and frisked about
him, attended with the Satyrs and their elders, the
Sileni. He had also the power of striking terrors,
especially such as were vain and superstitious ; whence
they came to be called panic terrors.

Few actions are recorded of him, only a principal
one is, that he challenged Cupid at wrestling, and was
worsted. He also catched the giant Typhon in a net,
and held him fast. They relate farther of him, that
when Ceres, growing disconsolate for the rape of Pros-
perine, hid herself, and all the gods took the utmost

pains to find her, by going out different ways for that purpose, Pan only had the good fortune to meet her, as he was hunting, and discovered her to the rest. He likewise had the assurance to rival Apollo in music; and in the judgment of Midas was preferred; but the judge had, though with great privacy and secrecy, a pair of ass's ears fastened on him for his sentence.

There is very little said of his amours; which may seem strange among such a multitude of gods, so profusely amorous. He is only reported to have been very fond of Echo, who was also esteemed his wife; and one nymph more, called Syrinx, with the love of whom Cupid inflamed him for his insolent challenge; so he is reported once to have solicited the moon to accompany him apart into the deep woods.

Lastly, Pan had no descendant, which also is a wonder, when the male gods were so extremely prolific; only he was the reputed father of a servant-girl called Iambe, who used to divert strangers with her ridiculous prattling stories.

This fable is perhaps the noblest of all antiquity, and pregnant with the mysteries and secrets of nature. Pan, as the name imports, represents the universe, about whose origin there are two opinions, viz., that it either sprung from Mercury, that is, the divine word, according to the Scriptures and philosophical divines, or from the confused seeds of things. For they who allow only one beginning of all things, either ascribe it to God; or, if they suppose a material beginning, acknowledge it to be various in its powers; so that the whole dispute comes to these points; namely, either that nature proceeds from Mercury, or from Penelope and all her suitors.

The third origin of Pan seems borrowed by the Greeks from the Hebrew mysteries, either by means of the Egyptians, or otherwise; for it relates to the state

of the world, not in its first creation, but as made
subject to death and corruption after the fall; and in
this state it was, and remains, the offspring of God and
Sin, or Jupiter and Reproach. And therefore these
three several accounts of Pan's birth may seem true,
if duly distinguished in respect of things and times.
For this Pan, or the universal nature of things, which
we view and contemplate, had its origin from the
divine Word and confused matter, first created by God
himself, with the subsequent introduction of sin, and
consequently corruption.

The Destinies, or the natures and fates of things, are
justly made Pan's sisters, as the chain of natural causes
links together the rise, duration, and corruption; the
exaltation, degeneration, and workings; the processes,
the effects, and changes, of all that can any way happen
to things.

Horns are given him, broad at the roots, but narrow
and sharp at the top, because the nature of all things
seems pyramidal; for individuals are infinite, but
being collected into a variety of species, they rise up
into kinds, and these again ascend, and are contracted
into generals, till at length nature may seem collected
to a point. And no wonder if Pan's horns reach to the
heavens, since the sublimities of nature, or abstract
ideas, reach in a manner to things divine; for there is
a short and ready passage from metaphysics to natural
theology.

Pan's body, or the body of nature, is, with great propriety and elegance, painted shaggy and hairy, as representing the rays of things; for rays are as the hair, or
fleece of nature, and more or less worn by all bodies.
This evidently appears in vision, and in all effects or
operations at a distance; for whatever operates thus
may be properly said to emit rays. But particularly
the beard of Pan is exceedingly long, because the rays

of the celestial bodies penetrate, and act to a prodigious distance, and have descended into the interior of the earth so far as to change its surface ; and the sun himself, when clouded on its upper part, appears to the eye bearded.

Again, the body of nature is justly described biform, because of the difference between its superior and inferior parts, as the former, for their beauty, regularity of motion, and influence over the earth, may be properly represented by the human figure, and the latter, because of their disorder, irregularity, and subjection to the celestial bodies, are by the brutal. This biform figure also represents the participation of one species with another ; for there appear to be no simple natures ; but all participate or consist of two : thus man has somewhat of the brute, the brute somewhat of the plant, the plant somewhat of the mineral ; so that all natural bodies have really two faces, or consist of a superior and an inferior species.

There lies a curious allegory in the making of Pan goatfooted, on account of the motion of ascent which the terrestrial bodies have towards the air and heavens ; for the goat is a clambering creature, that delights in climbing up rocks and precipices ; and in the same manner the matters destined to this lower globe strongly affect to rise upwards, as appears from the clouds and meteors.

Pan's arms, or the ensigns he bears in his hands, are of two kinds—the one an emblem of harmony, the other of empire. His pipe, composed of seven reeds, plainly denotes the consent and harmony, or the concords and discords of things, produced by the motion of the seven planets. His crook also contains a fine representation of the ways of nature, which are partly straight and partly crooked ; thus the staff, having an extraordinary bend towards the top, denotes that the works of Divine Providence are generally brought about by remote means, or in a circuit, as if somewhat else were intended rather than the effect produced, as in the sending of Joseph into Egypt, etc. So likewise in human government, they who sit at the helm manage and wind the people more successfully by pretext and oblique courses, than they could by such as are direct and straight ; so that, in effect, all sceptres are crooked at the top.

Pan's mantle, or clothing, is with great ingenuity made of a leopard's skin, because of the spots it has ; for in like manner the heavens are sprinkled with stars, the sea with islands, the earth with flowers, and almost each particular thing is variegated, or wears a mottled coat.

The office of Pan could not be more livelily expressed than by making him the god of hunters ; for every natural action, every motion and process, is no other than a chase : thus arts and sciences hunt out their works, and human schemes and counsels their several ends ; and all living creatures either hunt out their aliment, pursue their prey, or seek their pleasures, and this in a skilful and sagacious manner. He is also styled the god of the rural inhabitants, because men in this situation live more according to nature than they do in cities and courts, where nature is so corrupted with effeminate arts, that the saying of the poet may be verified—

——pars minima est ipsa puella sui.

He is likewise particularly styled President of the Mountains, because in mountains and lofty places the nature of things lies more open and exposed to the eye and the understanding.

In his being called the messenger of the gods, next after Mercury, lies a divine allegory, as next after the

Word of God, the image of the world is the herald of the Divine power and wisdom, according to the expression of the Psalmist, "The heavens declare the glory of God, and the firmament showeth his handiwork."

Pan is delighted with the company of the Nymphs ; that is, the souls of all living creatures are the delight of the world ; and he is properly called their governor, because each of them follows its own nature as a leader, and all dance about their own respective rings, with infinite variety and never-ceasing motion. And with these continually join the Satyrs and Sileni ; that is, youth and age : for all things have a kind of young, cheerful, and dancing time ; and again their time of slowness, tottering, and creeping. And whoever, in a true light, considers the motions and endeavors of both these ages, like another Democritus, will perhaps find them as odd and strange as the gesticulations and antic motions of the Satyrs and Sileni.

The power he had of striking terrors contains a very sensible doctrine ; for nature has implanted fear in all living creatures ; as well to keep them from risking their lives, as to guard against injuries and violence ; and yet this nature or passion keeps not its bounds, but with just and profitable fears always mixes such as are vain and senseless ; so that all things, if we could see their insides, would appear full of panic terrors. Thus mankind, particularly the vulgar, labor under a high degree of superstition, which is nothing more than a panic-dread that principally reigns in unsettled and troublesome times.

The presumption of Pan in challenging Cupid to the conflict, denotes that matter has an appetite and tendency to a dissolution of the world, and falling back to its first chaos again, unless this depravity and inclination were restrained and subdued by a more powerful concord and agreement of things, properly expressed by Love or Cupid ; it is therefore well for mankind, and the state of all things, that Pan was thrown and conquered in the struggle.

His catching and detaining Typhon in the net receives a similar explanation ; for whatever vast and unusual swells, which the word typhon signifies, may sometimes be raised in nature, as in the sea, the clouds, the earth, or the like, yet nature catches, entangles, and holds all such outrages and insurrections in her inextricable net, wove as it were of adamant.

That part of the fable which attributes the discovery of lost Ceres to Pan whilst he was hunting—a happiness denied the other gods, though they diligently and expressly sought her—contains an exceeding just and prudent admonition ; namely, that we are not to expect the discovery of things useful in common life, as that of corn, denoted by Ceres, from abstract philosophies, as if these were the gods of the first order,—no, not though we used our utmost endeavors this way,—but only from Pan, that is a sagacious experience and general knowledge of nature, which is often found, even by accident, to stumble upon such discoveries whilst the pursuit was directed another way.

The event of his contending with Apollo in music affords us a useful instruction, that may help to humble the human reason and judgment, which is too apt to boast and glory in itself. There seem to be two kinds of harmony—the one of Divine Providence, the other of human reason ; but the government of the world, the administration of its affairs, and the more secret Divine judgments, sound harsh and dissonant to human ears or human judgment ; and though this ignorance be justly rewarded with asses ears, yet they are put on and worn, not openly, but with great secrecy ; nor is the deformity of the thing seen or observed by the vulgar.

We must not find it strange if no amors are related
of Pan besides his marriage with Echo ; for nature
enjoys itself, and in itself all other things. He that
loves desires enjoyment, but in profusion there is no
room for desire ; and therefore Pan, remaining content
with himself, has no passion unless it be for discourse,
which is well shadowed out by Echo or talk, or when
it is more accurate, by Syrinx or writing. But Echo
makes a most excellent wife for Pan, as being no other
than genuine philosophy, which faithfully repeats his
words, or only transcribes exactly as nature dictates ;
thus representing the true image and reflection of the
world without adding a tittle.

It tends also to the support and perfection of Pan or
nature to be without offspring ; for the world generates
in its parts, and not in the way of a whole, as wanting
a body external to itself wherewith to generate.

Lastly, for the supposed or spurious prattling daughter
of Pan, it is an excellent addition to the fable, and
aptly represents the talkative philosophies that have at
all times been stirring, and filled the word with idle
tales, being ever barren, empty, and servile, though
sometimes indeed diverting and entertaining, and
sometimes again troublesome and importunate.

VII.—PERSEUS : OR WAR.

EXPLAINED OF THE PREPARATION AND CONDUCT NECESSARY TO WAR.

" The fable relates, that Perseus was despatched from
the east by Pallas, to cut off Medusa's head, who had
committed great ravage upon the people of the west ;
for this Medusa was so dire a monster as to turn into

stone all those who but looked upon her. She was a
Gorgon, and the only mortal one of the three, the other
two being invulnerable. Perseus, therefore, preparing
himself for this grand enterprise, had presents made
him from three of the gods : Mercury gave him wings
for his heels ; Pluto, a helmet ; and Pallas, a shield
and a mirror. But though he was now so well
equipped, he posted not directly to Medusa, but first
turned aside to the Greæ, who were half-sisters to the
Gorgons. These Greæ were gray-headed, and like old
women from their birth, having among them all three
but one eye, and one tooth, which as they had occasion
to go out, they each wore by turns, and laid them down
again upon coming back. This eye and this tooth they
lent to Perseus, who now judging himself sufficiently
furnished, he, without further stop, flies swiftly away
to Medusa, and finds her asleep. But not venturing his
eyes, for fear she should wake, he turned his head
aside, and viewed her in Pallas's mirror; and thus
directing his stroke, cut off her head ; when immediately, from the gushing blood, there darted
Pegasus, winged. Perseus now inserted Medusa's head
into Pallas's shield, which thence retained the faculty
of astonishing and benumbing all who looked on it."

This fable seems invented to show the prudent
method of choosing, undertaking, and conducting a
war ; and, accordingly, lays down three useful precepts
about it, as if they were the precepts of Pallas.

(1) The first is, that no prince should be over-
solicitous to subdue a neighboring nation ; for the
method of enlarging the empire is very different from
that of increasing an estate. Regard is justly had to
contiguity, or adjacency, in private lands and posses-
sions ; but in the extending of empire, the occasion,
the facility, and advantage of a war, are to be regarded
instead of vicinity. It is certain that the Romans, at

the time they stretched but little beyond Liguria to the west, had by their arms subdued the provinces as far as Mount Taurus to the east. And thus Perseus readily undertook a very long expedition, even from the east to the extremities of the west.

The second precept is, that the cause of the war be just and honorable ; for this adds alacrity both to the soldiers, and the people who find the supplies : procures aids, alliances, and numerous other conveniences. Now there is no cause of war more just and laudable than the suppressing of tyranny, by which a people are dispirited, benumbed, or left without life and vigor, as at the sight of Medusa.

Lastly, it is prudently added, that as there were three of the Gorgons, who represent war, Perseus singled her out for his expedition that was mortal ; which affords this precept, that such kind of wars should be chose as may be brought to a conclusion, without pursuing vast and infinite hopes.

Again, Perseus's setting-out is extremely well adapted to his undertaking, and in a manner commands success ; he received despatch from Mercury, secrecy from Pluto, and foresight from Pallas. It also contains an excellent allegory, that the wings given him by Mercury were for his heels, not for his shoulders ; because expedition is not so much required in the first preparations for war, as in the subsequent matters, that administer to the first ; for there is no error more frequent in war, than, after brisk preparations, to halt for subsidiary forces and effective supplies.

The allegory of Pluto's helmet, rendering men invisible and secret, is sufficiently evident of itself ; but the mystery of the shield and the mirror lies deeper, and denotes, that not only a prudent caution must be had to defend, like the shield, but also such an address and penetration as may discover the strength, the motions, the counsels, and designs of the enemy ; like the mirror of Pallas.

But though Perseus may now seem extremely well prepared, there still remains the most important thing of all ; before he enters upon the war, he must of necessity consult the Greæ. These Greæ are treasons ; half, but degenerate sisters of the Gorgons ; who are representatives of wars : for wars are generous and noble ; but treasons base and vile. The Greæ are elegantly described as hoary-headed, and like old women from their birth ; on account of the perpetual cares, fears, and trepidations attending traitors. Their force, also, before it breaks out into open revolt, consists either in an eye or a tooth ; for all faction alienated from a state, is both watchful and biting ; and this eye and tooth are, as it were, common to all the disaffected ; because whatever they learn and know is transmitted from one to another, as by the hands of faction. And for the tooth, they all bite with the same ; and clamor with one throat; so that each of them singly expresses the multitude.

These Greæ, therefore, must be prevailed upon by Perseus to lend him their eye and their tooth ; the eye to give him indications, and make discoveries ; the tooth for sowing rumors, raising envy, and stirring up the minds of the people. And when all these things are thus disposed and prepared, then follows the action of the war.

He finds Medusa asleep; for whoever undertakes a war with prudence, generally falls upon the enemy unprepared, and nearly in a state of security; and here is the occasion for Pallas's mirror : for it is common enough, before the danger presents itself, to see exactly into the state and posture of the enemy; but the principal use of the glass is, in the very instant of danger, to discover the manner thereof, and prevent consternation; which is the thing intended by Perseus's turning his head aside, and viewing the enemy in the glass.

Two effects here follow the conquest : 1. The darting forth of Pegasus; which evidently denotes fame, that flies abroad, proclaiming the victory far and near. 2. The bearing of Medusa's head in the shield, which is the greatest possible defence and safeguard ; for one grand and memorable enterprise, happily accomplished, bridles all the motions and attempts of the enemy, stupifies disaffections, and quells commotions.

VIII.—ENDYMION : OR A FAVORITE.

EXPLAINED OF COURT FAVORITES.

The goddess Luna is said to have fallen in love with the shepherd Endymion, and to have carried on her amours with him in a new and singular manner ; it being her custom, whilst he lay reposing in his native cave, under Mount Latmus, to descend frequently from her sphere, enjoy his company whilst he slept, and then go up to heaven again. And all this while Endymion's fortune was no way prejudiced by his unactive and sleepy life, the goddess causing his flocks to thrive, and grow so exceeding numerous, that none of the other shepherds could compare with him.

Explanation.—This fable seems to describe the tempers and dispositions of princes, who, being thoughtful and suspicious, do not easily admit to their privacies such men as are prying, curious, and vigilant, or, as it were, sleepless; but rather such as are of an easy, obliging nature, and indulge them in their pleasures, without seeking anything farther ; but seeming ignorant, insensible, or, as it were, lulled asleep before them. Princes usually treat such persons familiarly ; and, quitting their throne like Luna, think they may with safety unbosom to them. This temper was very remarkable in Tiberius, a prince exceeding difficult to please, and who had no favorites but those that perfectly understood his way, and, at the same time, obstinately dissembled their knowledge, almost to a degree of stupidity.

The cave is not improperly mentioned in the fable ; it being a common thing for the favorites of a prince to have their pleasant retreats, whither to invite him, by way of relaxation, though without prejudice to their own fortunes ; these favorites usually making a good provision for themselves.

For though their prince should not, perhaps, promote them to dignities, yet, out of real affection, and not only for convenience, they generally feel the enriching influence of his bounty.

IX.—THE SISTERS OF THE GIANTS: OR FAME.
EXPLAINED OF PUBLIC DETRACTION.

The poets relate, that the giants, produced from the earth, made war upon Jupiter, and the other gods, but were repulsed and conquered by thunder ; whereat the earth, provoked, brought forth Fame, the youngest sister of the giants, in revenge for the death of her sons.

Explanation.—The meaning of the fable seems to be this : the earth denotes the nature of the vulgar who are always swelling, and rising against their rulers, and endeavoring at changes. This disposition, getting a fit opportunity, breeds rebels and traitors, who, with impetuous rage, threaten and contrive the overthrow and destruction of princes.

And when brought under and subdued, the same vile and restless nature of the people, impatient of peace, produces rumors, detractions, slanders, libels, etc., to blacken those in authority ; so that rebellious actions and seditious rumors, differ not in origin and stock, but only as it were in sex ; treasons and rebellions being the brothers, and scandal or detraction the sister.

X.—ACTEON AND PENTHEUS: OR A CURIOUS MAN.

EXPLAINED OF CURIOSITY, OR PRYING INTO THE SECRETS OF PRINCES AND DIVINE MYSTERIES.

The ancients afford us two examples for suppressing the impertinent curiosity of mankind, in diving into secrets, and imprudently longing and endeavoring to discover them. The one of these is in the person of Acteon, and the other in that of Pentheus. Acteon, undesignedly chancing to see Diana naked, was turned into a stag, and torn to pieces by his own hounds. And Pentheus, desiring to pry into the hidden mysteries of Bacchus's sacrifice, and climbing a tree for that purpose, was struck with a phrensy. This phrensy of Pentheus caused him to see things double, particularly the sun, and his own city Thebes, so that running homewards, and immediately espying another Thebes, he runs towards that ; and thus continues incessantly tending first to the one, and then to the other, without coming at either.

Explanation.—The first of these fables may relate to the secrets of princes, and the second to divine mysteries. For they who are not intimate with a prince, yet against his will have a knowledge of his secrets, inevitably incur his displeasure ; and therefore, being aware that they are singled out, and all opportunities watched against them, they lead the life of a stag, full of fears and suspicions. It likewise frequently happens that their servants and domestics accuse them, and plot their overthrow, in order to procure favor with the prince ; for whenever the king manifests his displeasure, the person it falls upon must expect his servants to betray him, and worry him down, as Acteon was worried by his own dogs.

The punishment of Pentheus is of another kind ; for they who, unmindful of their mortal state, rashly aspire to divine mysteries, by climbing the heights of nature and philosophy, here represented by climbing a tree,—their fate is perpetual inconstancy, perplexity, and instability of judgment. For as there is one light of nature, and another light that is divine, they see, as it were, two suns. And as the actions of life, and the determinations of the will, depend upon the understanding, they are distracted as much in opinion as in will; and therefore judge very inconsistently, or contradictorily ; and see, as it were, Thebes double ; for Thebes, being the refuge and habitation of Pentheus, here denotes the ends of actions : whence they know not what course to take, but remaining undetermined and unresolved in their views and designs, they are merely driven about by every sudden gust and impulse of the mind.

XI.—ORPHEUS : OR PHILOSOPHY.

EXPLAINED OF NATURAL AND MORAL PHILOSOPHY.

Introduction.—The fable of Orpheus, though trite and common, has never been well interpreted, and seems to hold out a picture of universal philosophy ; for to this sense may be easily transferred what is said of his being a wonderful and perfectly divine person, skilled in all kinds of harmony, subduing and drawing all things after him by sweet and gentle methods and modulations. For the labors of Orpheus exceed the labors of Hercules, both in power and dignity, as the works of knowledge exceed the works of strength.

Fable.—Orpheus having his beloved wife snatched from him by sudden death, resolved upon descending to the infernal regions, to try if, by the power of his harp, he could re-obtain her. And, in effect, he so appeased and soothed the infernal powers by the melody and sweetness of his harp and voice, that they indulged him the liberty of taking her back, on condition that she should follow him behind, and he not turn to look upon her till they came into open day ; but he, through the impatience of his care and affection, and thinking himself almost past danger, at length looked behind him, whereby the condition was violated, and she again precipitated to Pluto's regions. From this time Orpheus grew pensive and sad, a hater of the sex, and went into solitude, where, by the same sweetness of his harp and voice, he first drew the wild beasts of all sorts about him ; so that, forgetting their natures, they were neither actuated by revenge, cruelty, lust, hunger, or the desire of prey, but stood gazing about him, in a tame and gentle manner, listening attentively to his music. Nay, so great was the power and efficacy of his harmony, that it even caused

the trees and stones to remove, and place themselves
in a regular manner about him. When he had for a
time, and with great admiration, continued to do this,
at length the Thracian women, raised by the instigation
of Bacchus, first blew a deep and hoarse-sounding
horn, in such an outrageous manner, that it quite
drowned the music of Orpheus. And thus the power
which, as the link of their society, held all things in
order, being dissolved, disturbance reigned anew ;
each creature returned to its own nature, and pursued
and preyed upon its fellow, as before. The rocks and
woods also started back to their former places ; and
even Orpheus himself was at last torn to pieces by
these female furies, and his limbs scattered all over
the desert. But, in sorrow and revenge for his death,
the river Helicon, sacred to the Muses, hid its waters
under ground, and rose again in other places.

Explanation.—The fable receives this explanation.
The music of Orpheus is of two kinds ; one that
appeases the infernal powers, and the other that draws
together the wild beasts and trees. The former properly relates to natural, and the latter to moral
philosophy, or civil society. The reinstatement and
restoration of corruptible things is the noblest work of
natural philosophy ; and, in a less degree, the preser-
vation of bodies in their own state, or a prevention of
their dissolution and corruption. And if this be
possible, it can certainly be effected no other way than
by proper and exquisite attemperations of nature ; as
it were by the harmony and fine touching of the harp.
But as this is a thing of exceeding great difficulty, the
end is seldom obtained ; and that, probably, for no
reason more than a curious and unseasonable impatience and solicitude.

And, therefore, philosophy, being almost unequal to
the task, has cause to grow sad, and hence betakes

itself to human affairs, insinuating into men's minds the love of virtue, equity, and peace, by means of eloquence and persuasion ; thus forming men into societies ; bringing them under laws and regulations ; and making them forget their unbridled passions and affections, so long as they hearken to precepts and submit to discipline. And thus they soon after build themselves habitations, form cities, cultivate lands, plant orchards, gardens, etc. So that they may not improperly be said to remove and call the trees and stones together.

And this regard to civil affairs is justly and regularly placed after diligent trial made for restoring the mortal body ; the attempt being frustrated in the end— because the unavoidable necessity of death, thus evidently laid before mankind, animates them to seek a kind of eternity by works of perpetuity, character, and fame.

It is also prudently added, that Orpheus was afterwards averse to women and wedlock, because the indulgence of a married state, and the natural affections which men have for their children, often prevent them from entering upon any grand, noble, or meritorious enterprise for the public good ; as thinking it sufficient to obtain immortality by their descendants, without endeavoring at great actions.

And even the works of knowledge, though the most excellent among human things, have their periods ; for after kingdoms and commonwealths have flourished for a time, disturbances, seditions, and wars, often arise, in the din whereof, first the laws are silent and not heard ; and then men return to their own depraved natures—whence cultivated lands and cities soon become desolate and waste. And if this disorder continues, learning and philosophy is infallibly torn to pieces ; so that only some scattered fragments thereof

c

can afterwards be found up and down, in a few places, like planks after a shipwreck. And barbarous times succeeding, the river Helicon dips under-ground ; that is, letters are buried, till things having undergone their due course of changes, learning rises again, and shows its head, though seldom in the same place, but in some other nation.

XII.—CŒLUM : OR BEGINNINGS.

EXPLAINED OF THE CREATION, OR ORIGIN OF ALL THINGS.

The poets relate, that Cœlum was the most ancient of all the gods ; that his parts of generation were cut off by his son Saturn ; that Saturn had a numerous offspring, but devoured all his sons, as soon as they were born ; that Jupiter at length escaped the common fate ; and when grown up, drove his father Saturn into Tartarus ; usurped the kingdom ; cut off his father's genitals, with the same knife wherewith Saturn had dismembered Cœlum, and throwing them into the sea, thence sprung Venus.

Before Jupiter was well established in his empire. two memorable wars were made upon him : the first by the Titans, in subduing of whom Sol, the only one of the Titans who favored Jupiter, performed him singular service ; the second by the giants, who being destroyed and subdued by the thunder and arms of Jupiter, he now reigned secure.

Explanation.—This fable appears to be an enigmatical account of the origin of all things, not greatly differing from the philosophy afterwards embraced by Democritus, who expressly asserts the eternity of matter, but denies the eternity of the world ; thereby approaching to the truth of sacred writ, which makes chaos, or uninformed matter, to exist before the six days' works.

The meaning of the fable seems to be this : Cœlum denotes the concave space, or vaulted roof that incloses all matter, and Saturn the matter itself, which cuts off all power of generation from his father ; as one and the same quantity of matter remains invariable in nature, without addition or diminution. But the agitations and struggling motions of matter first produced certain imperfect and ill-joined compositions of things, as it were so many first rudiments, or essays of worlds ; till, in process of time, there arose a fabric capable of preserving its form and structure. Whence the first age was shadowed out by the reign of Saturn ; who, on account of the frequent dissolutions, and short durations of things, was said to devour his children. And the second age was denoted by the reign of Jupiter ; who thrust, or drove those frequent and transitory changes into Tartarus—a place expressive of disorder. This place seems to be in the middle space, between the lower heavens and the internal parts of the earth, wherein disorder, imperfection, mutation, mortality, destruction. and corruption, are principally found.

Venus was not born during the former generation of things, under the reign of Saturn ; for whilst discord and jar had the upper hand of concord and uniformity in the matter of the universe, a change of the entire structure was necessary. And in this manner things were generated and destroyed, before Saturn was dismembered. But when this manner of generation ceased, there immediately followed another, brought about by Venus, or a perfect and established harmony of things ; whereby changes were wrought in the parts, whilst the universal fabric remained entire and undisturbed. Saturn, however, is said to be thrust out and dethroned, not killed, and become extinct; because, agreeably to the opinion of Democritus, the world might relapse into its old confusion and disorder, which Lucretius hoped would not happen in his time.

But now, when the world was compact, and held together by its own bulk and energy, yet there was no rest from the beginning; for first, there followed considerable motions and disturbances in the celestial regions, though so regulated and moderated by the power of the Sun, prevailing over the heavenly bodies, as to continue the world in its state. Afterwards there followed the like in the lower parts, by inundations, storms, winds, general earthquakes, etc., which, however, being subdued and kept under, there ensued a more peaceable and lasting harmony, and consent of things.

It may be said of this fable, that it includes philosophy; and again, that philosophy includes the fable; for we know, by faith, that all these things are but the oracle of sense, long since ceased and decayed; but the matter and fabric of the world being justly attributed to a creator.

XIII.—PROTEUS: OR MATTER.

EXPLAINED OF MATTER AND ITS CHANGES.

Proteus, according to the poets, was Neptune's herdsman: an old man, and a most extraordinary prophet, who understood things past and present, as well as future: so that besides the business of divination, he was the revealer and interpreter of all antiquity, and secrets of every kind. He lived in a vast cave, where his custom was to tell over his herd of sea-calves at noon, and then to sleep. Whoever consulted him had no other way of obtaining an answer but by binding him with manacles and fetters ; when he, endeavoring to free himself, would change into all kinds of shapes and miraculous forms ; as of fire, water, wild beasts, etc. ; till at length he resumed his own shape again.

Explanation.—This fable seems to point at the secrets of nature, and the states of matter. For the person of Proteus denotes matter, the oldest of all things, after God himself ; that resides, as in a cave, under the vast concavity of the heavens. He is represented as the servant of Neptune, because the various operations and modifications of matter are principally wrought in a fluid state. The herd, or flock of Proteus, seems to be no other than the several kinds of animals, plants, and minerals, in which matter appears to diffuse and spend itself; so that after having formed these several species, and as it were finished its task, it seems to sleep and repose, without otherwise attempting to produce any new ones. And this is the moral of Proteus's counting his herd, then going to sleep.

This is said to be done at noon, not in the morning or evening ; by which is meant the time best fitted and disposed for the production of species, from a matter duly prepared, and made ready beforehand, and now lying in a middle state, between its first rudiments and decline ; which, we learn from sacred history, was the case at the time of the creation ; when, by the efficacy of the divine command, matter directly came together, without any transformation or intermediate changes, which it affects ; instantly obeyed the order, and appeared in the form of creatures.

And thus far the fable reaches of Proteus, and his flock, at liberty and unrestrained. For the universe, with the common structures and fabrics of the creatures, is the face of matter, not under constraint, or as the flock wrought upon and tortured by human means. But if any skilful minister of nature shall apply force to matter, and by design torture and vex it, in order to its annihilation, it, on the contrary, being brought under this necessity, changes and transforms itself into a strange variety of shapes and appearances; for nothing but the power of the Creator can annihilate, or truly destroy it; so that at length, running through the whole circle of transformations, and completing its period, it in some degree restores itself, if the force be continued. And that method of binding, torturing, or detaining, will prove the most effectual and expeditious, which makes use of manacles and fetters; that is, lays hold and works upon matter in the extremest degrees.

The addition in the fable that makes Proteus a prophet, who had the knowledge of things past, present, and future, excellently agrees with the nature of matter; as he who knows the properties, the changes, and the processes of matter, must of necessity understand the effects and sum of what it does, has done, or can do, though his knowledge extends not to all the parts and particulars thereof.

XIV.—MEMNON: OR A YOUTH TOO FORWARD.

EXPLAINED OF THE FATAL PRECIPITANCY OF YOUTH.

The poets made Memnon the son of Aurora, and bring him to the Trojan war in beautiful armor, and flushed with popular praise; where, thirsting after farther glory, and rashly hurrying on to the greatest enterprises, he engages the bravest warrior of all the

Greeks, Achilles, and falls by his hand in single combat. Jupiter, in commisseration of his death, sent birds to grace his funeral, that perpetually chanted certain mournful and bewailing dirges. It is also reported, that the rays of the rising sun, striking his statue, used to give a lamenting sound.

Explanation.—This fable regards the unfortunate end of those promising youths, who, like sons of the morning, elate with empty hopes and glittering out-sides, attempt things beyond their strength : challenge the bravest heroes ; provoke them to the combat ; and proving unequal, die in their high attempts.

The death of such youths seldom fails to meet with infinite pity ; as no mortal calamity is more moving and afflicting, than to see the flower of virtue cropped before its time. Nay, the prime of life enjoyed to the full, or even to a degree of envy, does not assuage or moderate the grief occasioned by the untimely death of such hopeful youths ; but lamentations and bewailings fly, like mournful birds, about their tombs, for a long while after ; especially upon all fresh occasions, new commotions, and the beginning of great actions, the passionate desire of them is renewed, as by the sun's morning rays.

XV.—TYTHONUS : OR SATIETY.
EXPLAINED OF PREDOMINANT PASSIONS.

It is elegantly fabled by Tythonus, that being exceed-ingly beloved by Aurora, she petitioned Jupiter that he might prove immortal, thereby to secure herself the everlasting enjoyment of his company ; but through female inadvertence she forgot to add, that he might never grow old ; so that, though he proved immortal, he became miserably worn and consumed with age, insomuch that Jupiter, out of pity, at length transformed him to a grasshopper.

Explanation.—This fable seems to contain an ingenious description of pleasure ; which at first, as it were, in the morning of the day, is so welcome, that men pray to have it everlasting, but forget that satiety and weariness of it will, like old age, overtake them, though they think not of it ; so that at length, when their appetite for pleasurable actions is gone, their desires and affections often continue ; whence we commonly find that aged persons delight themselves with the discourse and remembrance of the things agreeable to them in their better days. This is very remarkable in men of a loose, and men of a military life ; the former whereof are always talking over their amours, and the latter the exploits of their youth ; like grasshoppers, that show their vigor only by their chirping.

XVI.—JUNO'S SUITOR : OR BASENESS.
EXPLAINED OF SUBMISSION AND ABJECTION.

The poets tell us, that Jupiter, to carry on his love intrigues, assumed many different shapes ; as of a bull, an eagle, a swan, a golden shower, etc. ; but when he attempted Juno, he turned himself into the most ignoble and ridiculous creature—even that of a wretched, wet, weather-beaten, affrighted, trembling, and half-starved cuckoo.

Explanation.—This a wise fable, and drawn from the very entrails of morality. The moral is, that men should not be conceited of themselves, and imagine that a discovery of their excellences will always render them acceptable; for this can only succeed according to the nature and manners of the person they court, or solicit ; who, if he be a man not of the same gifts and endowments, but altogether of a haughty and contemptuous behavior, here represented by the person of Juno, they must entirely drop the character that carries the least show of worth, or gracefulness ; if they proceed upon any other footing, it is downright folly ; nor is it sufficient to act the deformity of obsequiousness, unless they really change themselves, and become abject and contemptible in their persons.

XVII.—CUPID : OR AN ATOM.
EXPLAINED OF THE CORPUSCULAR PHILOSOPHY.

The particulars related by the poets of Cupid, or Love, do not properly agree to the same person ; yet they differ only so far, that if the confusion of persons be rejected, the correspondence may hold. They say, that Love was the most ancient of all the gods, and existed before everything else, except Chaos, which is held coeval therewith. But for Chaos, the ancients never paid divine honors, nor gave the title of a god thereto. Love is represented absolutely without progenitor, excepting only that he is said to have proceeded from the egg of Nox ; but that himself begot the gods, and all things else, on Chaos. His attributes are four, viz.—1, perpetual infancy ; 2, blindness ; 3, nakedness ; and 4, archery.

There was also another Cupid, or Love, the youngest son of the gods, born of Venus ; and upon him the attributes of the elder are transferred, with some degree of correspondence.

Explanation.—This fable points at, and enters, the cradle of nature. Love seems to be the appetite, or incentive, of the primitive matter; or, to speak more distinctly, the natural motion, or moving principle, of the original corpuscles, or atoms; this being the most ancient and only power that made and wrought all things out of matter. It is absolutely without parent, that is, without cause : for causes are as parents to effects ; but this power or efficacy could have no natural cause ; for, excepting God, nothing was before it ; and therefore it could have no efficient in nature. And as nothing is more inward with nature, it can neither be a genus nor a form ; and therefore, whatever it is, it must be somewhat positive, though inexpressible. And if it were possible to conceive its modus and process, yet it could not be known from its cause, as being, next to God, the cause of causes, and itself without a cause. And perhaps we are not to hope that the modus of it should fall, or be comprehended, under human inquiry. Whence it is properly feigned to be the egg of Nox, or laid in the dark.

The divine philosopher declares, that "God has made everything beautiful in its season ; and has given over the world to our disputes and inquiries : but that man cannot find out the work which God has wrought, from its beginning up to its end." Thus the summary or collective law of nature, or the principle of love, impressed by God upon the original particles of all things, so as to make them attack each other and come together, by the repetition and multiplication whereof all the variety in the universe is produced, can scarce possibly find full admittance into the thoughts of men, though some faint notion may be had thereof. The Greek philosophy is subtile, and busied in discovering the material principles of things, but negligent and languid in discovering the principles of motion, in which the energy and efficacy of every operation consists. And here the Greek philosophers seem perfectly blind and childish ; for the opinion of the Peripatetics, as to the stimulus of matter, by privation, is little more than words, or rather sound than signification. And they who refer it to God, though they do well therein, yet they do it by a start, and not by proper degrees of assent ; for doubtless there is one summary, or capital law, in which nature meets, subordinate to God, viz., the law mentioned in the passage above quoted from Solomon ; or the work which God has wrought from its beginning up to its end.

Democritus, who farther considered this subject, having first supposed an atom, or corpuscle, of some dimension or figure, attributed thereto an appetite, desire, or first motion simply, and another comparatively, imagining that all things properly tended to the centre of the world ; those containing more matter falling faster to the centre, and thereby removing, and in the shock driving away, such as held less. But this is a slender conceit, and regards too few particulars ; for neither the revolutions of the celestial bodies, nor the contractions and expansions of things, can be reduced to this principle. And for the opinion of Epicurus, as to the declination and fortuitous agitation of atoms, this only brings the matter back again to a trifle, and wraps it up in ignorance and night.

Cupid is elegantly drawn a perpetual child ; for compounds are larger things, and have their periods of age ; but the first seeds or atoms of bodies are small, and remain in a perpetual infant state.

He is again justly represented naked ; as all compounds may properly be said to be dressed and clothed, or to assume a personage ; whence nothing remains truly naked, but the original particles of things.

The blindness of Cupid, contains a deep allegory ; for this same Cupid, Love, or appetite of the world, seems to have very little foresight, but directs his steps and motions conformably to what he finds next him, as blind men do when they feel out their way ; which renders the divine and over-ruling Providence and foresight the more surprising ; as by a certain steady law, it brings such a beautiful order and regularity of things out of what seems extremely casual, void of design, and, as it were, really blind.

The last attribute of Cupid is archery, viz., a virtue or power operating at a distance ; for everything that operates at a distance, may seem, as it were, to dart, or shoot with arrows. And whoever allows of atoms and vacuity, necessarily supposes that the virtue of atoms operates at a distance ; for without this operation, no motion could be excited, on account of the vacuum interposing, but all things would remain sluggish and unmoved.

As to the other Cupid, he is properly said to be the youngest sons of the gods, as his power could not take place before the formation of species, or particular bodies. The description given us of him transfers the allegory to morality, though he still retains some resemblance with the ancient Cupid ; for as Venus universally excites the affection of association, and the desire of procreation, her son Cupid applies the affection to individuals ; so that the general disposition proceeds from Venus, but the more close sympathy from Cupid. The former depends upon a near approximation of causes, but the latter upon deeper, more necessitating and uncontrollable principles, as if they proceeded from the ancient Cupid, on whom all exquisite sympathies depend.

XVIII.—DIOMED : OR ZEAL.

EXPLAINED OF PERSECUTION, OR ZEAL FOR RELIGION.

Diomed acquired great glory and honor at the Trojan war, and was highly favored by Pallas, who encouraged and excited him by no means to spare Venus, if he should casually meet her in fight. He followed the advice with too much eagerness and intrepidity, and accordingly wounded that goddess in her hand. This presumptuous action remained unpunished for a time, and when the war was ended he returned with great glory and renown to his own country, where, finding himself embroiled with domestic affairs, he retired into Italy. Here also at first he was well received and nobly entertained by King Daunus, who, besides other gifts and honors, erected statues for him over all his dominions. But upon the first calamity that afflicted the people after the stranger's arrival, Daunus immediately reflected that he entertained a devoted person in his palace, an enemy to the gods, and one who had sacrilegiously wounded a goddess with his sword, whom it was impious but to touch. To expiate, therefore, his country's guilt, he, without regard to the laws of hospitality, which were less regarded by him than the laws of religion, directly slew his guest, and commanded his statues and all his honors to be razed and abolished. Nor was it safe for others to commiserate or bewail so cruel a destiny ; but even his companions in arms, whilst they lamented the death of their leader, and filled all places with their complaints, were turned into a kind of swans, which are said, at the approach of their own death, to chant sweet melancholy dirges.

Explanation.—This fable intimates an extraordinary and almost singular thing, for no hero besides Diomed is recorded to have wounded any of the gods. Doubtless we have here described the nature and fate of a man who professedly makes any divine worship or sect of religion, though in itself vain and light, the only scope of his actions, and resolves to propagate it by fire and sword. For although the bloody dissensions and differences about religion were unknown to the ancients, yet so copious and diffusive was their knowledge, that what they knew not by experience they comprehended in thought and representation. Those, therefore, who endeavor to reform or establish any sect of religion, though vain, corrupt, or infamous (which is here denoted under the person of Venus), not by the force of reason, learning, sanctity of manners, the weight of arguments, and examples, but would spread or extirpate it by persecution, pains, penalties, tortures, fire and sword, may perhaps be instigated hereto by Pallas, that is, by a certain rigid, prudential consideration, and a severity of judgment, by the vigor and efficacy whereof they see thoroughly into the fallacies and fictions of the delusions of this kind; and through aversion to depravity and a well-meant zeal, these men usually for a time acquire great fame and glory, and are by the vulgar, to whom no moderate measures can be acceptable, extolled and almost adored, as the only patrons and protectors of truth and religion, men of any other disposition seeming, in comparison with these, to be lukewarm, mean-spirited, and cowardly. This fame and felicity, however, seldom endures to the end; but all violence, unless it escapes the reverses and changes of things by untimely death, is commonly unprosperous in the issue; and if a change of affairs happens, and that sect of religion which was persecuted and oppressed gains strength and rises again, then the zeal and warm endeavors of this sort of men are condemned, their very name becomes odious, and all their honors terminate in disgrace.

As to the point that Diomed should be slain by his hospitable entertainer, this denotes that religious dissensions may cause treachery, bloody animosities, and deceit, even between the nearest friends.

That complaining or bewailing should not, in so enormous a case, be permitted to friends affected by the catastrophe without punishment, includes this prudent admonition, that almost in all kinds of wickedness and depravity men have still room left for commiseration, so that they who hate the crime may yet pity the person and bewail his calamity, from a principle of humanity and good nature ; and to forbid the overflowings and intercourses of pity upon such occasions were the extremest of evils ; yet in the cause of religion and impiety the very commiserations of men are noted and suspected. On the other hand, the lamentations and complainings of the followers and attendants of Diomed, that is, of men of the same sect or persuasion, are usually very sweet, agreeable, and moving, like the dying notes of swans, or the birds of Diomed. This is also a noble and remarkable part of the allegory, denoting that the last words of those who suffer for the sake of religion strongly affect and sway men's minds, and leave a lasting impression upon the sense and memory.

XIX.—DÆDALUS : OR MECHANICAL SKILL.

EXPLAINED OF ARTS AND ARTISTS IN KINGDOMS AND STATES.

The ancients have left us a description of mechanical skill, industry, and curious arts converted to ill uses, in the person of Dædalus, a most ingenious but execrable artist. This Dædalus was banished for the

murder of his brother artist and rival, yet found a kind
reception in his banishment from the kings and states
where he came. He raised many incomparable edifices
to the honor of the gods, and invented many new con-
trivances for the beautifying and ennobling of cities
and public places, but still he was most famous for
wicked inventions. Among the rest, by his abominable
industry and destructive genius, he assisted in the fatal
and infamous production of the monster Minotaur,
that devourer of promising youths. And then, to
cover one mischief with another, and provide for the
security of this monster, he invented and built a
labyrinth ; a work infamous for its end and design,
but admirable and prodigious for art and workmanship.
After this, that he might not only be celebrated for
wicked inventions, but be sought after, as well for
prevention, as for instruments of mischief, he formed
that ingenious device of his clue, which led directly
through all the windings of the labyrinth. This
Dædalus was persecuted by Minos with the utmost
severity, diligence, and inquiry ; but he always found
refuge and means of escaping. Lastly, endeavoring to
teach his son Icarus the art of flying, the novice,
trusting too much to his wings, fell from his towering
flight, and was drowned in the sea.

Explanation.—The sense of the fable runs thus.
It first denotes envy, which is continually upon the
watch, and strangely prevails among excellent artificers ;
for no kind of people are observed to be more im-
placably and destructively envious to one another than
these.

In the next place, it observes an impolitic and improvident kind of punishment inflicted upon Dædalus
—that of banishment ; for good workmen are gladly
received everywhere, so that banishment to an excellent
artificer is scarce any punishment at all ; whereas other

conditions of life cannot easily flourish from home.
For the admiration of artists is propagated and increased
among foreigners and strangers ; it being a principle
in the minds of men to slight and despise the mechanical operators of their own nation.

The succeeding part of the fable is plain, concerning
the use of mechanical arts, whereto human life stands
greatly indebted, as receiving from this treasury
numerous particulars for the service of religion, the
ornament of civil society, and the whole provision and
apparatus of life ; but then the same magazine supplies
instruments of lust, cruelty, and death. For, not to
mention the arts of luxury and debauchery, we plainly
see how far the business of exquisite poisons, guns,
engines of war, and such kind of destructive inventions, exceeds the cruelty and barbarity of the Minotaur
himself.

The addition of the labyrinth contains a beautiful
allegory, representing the nature of mechanic arts in
general ; for all ingenious and accurate mechanical
inventions may be conceived as a labyrinth, which, by
reason of their subtilty, intricacy, crossing, and inter-
fering with one another, and the apparent resemblances
they have among themselves, scarce any power of the
judgment can unravel and distinguish ; so that they
are only to be understood and traced by the clue of
experience.

It is no less prudently added, that he who invented
the windings of the labyrinth, should also show the
use and management of the clue ; for mechanical arts
have an ambiguous or double use, and serve as well to
produce as to prevent mischief and destruction ; so
that their virtue almost destroys or unwinds itself.

Unlawful arts, and indeed frequently arts themselves,
are persecuted by Minos, that is, by laws, which prohibit and forbid their use among the people ; but

D

notwithstanding this, they are hid, concealed, retained, and everywhere find reception and skulking-places ; a thing well observed by Tacitus of the astrologers and fortune-tellers of his time. "These," says he, "are a kind of men that will always be prohibited, and yet will always be retained in our city."

But lastly, all unlawful and vain arts, of what kind soever, lose their reputation in tract of time ; grow contemptible and perish, through their over-confidence, like Icarus ; being commonly unable to perform what they boasted. And to say the truth, such arts are better suppressed by their own vain pretensions, than checked or restrained by the bridle of laws.

XX.—ERICTHONIUS : OR IMPOSTURE.

EXPLAINED OF THE IMPROPER USE OF FORCE IN NATURAL PHILOSOPHY.

The poets feign that Vulcan attempted the chastity of Minerva, and impatient of refusal, had recourse to force ; the consequence of which was the birth of Ericthonius, whose body from the middle upwards was comely and well-proportioned, but his thighs and legs small, shrunk, and deformed, like an eel. Conscious of this defect, he became the inventor of chariots, so as to show the graceful, but conceal the deformed part of his body.

Explanation.—This strange fable seems to carry this meaning. Art is here represented under the person of Vulcan, by reason of the various uses it makes of fire ; and nature under the person of Minerva, by reason of the industry employed in her works. Art, therefore, whenever it offers violence to nature, in order to conquer, subdue, and bend her to its purpose, by tortures and force of all kinds, seldom obtains the end proposed ; yet upon great struggle and application, there proceed certain imperfect births, or lame abortive works, specious in appearance, but weak and unstable in use ; which are, nevertheless, with great pomp and deceitful appearances, triumphantly carried about and shown by impostors. A procedure very familiar, and remarkable in chemical productions, and new mechanical inventions ; especially when the inventors rather hug their errors than improve upon them, and go on struggling with nature, not courting her.

XXI.—DEUCALION : OR RESTITUTION.

EXPLAINED OF A USEFUL HINT IN NATURAL PHILOSOPHY

The poets tell us that the inhabitants of the old world being totally destroyed by the universal deluge, excepting Deucalion and Pyrrha, these two, desiring with zealous and fervent devotion to restore mankind, received this oracle for answer, that "they should succeed by throwing their mother's bones behind them." This at first cast them into great sorrow and despair, because, as all things were levelled by the deluge, it was in vain to seek their mother's tomb ; but at length they understood the expression of the oracle to signify the stones of the earth, which is esteemed the mother of all things.

Explanation.—This fable seems to reveal a secret of nature, and correct an error familiar to the mind; for men's ignorance leads them to expect the renovation or restoration of things from their corruption and remains, as the phœnix is said to be restored out of its ashes ; which is a very improper procedure, because such kind of materials have finished their course, and are become absolutely unfit to supply the first rudiments of the same things again; whence, in cases of renovation, recourse should be had to more common principles.

XXII.—NEMESIS : OR THE VICISSITUDE OF THINGS.

EXPLAINED OF THE REVERSES OF FORTUNE.

Nemesis is represented as a goddess venerated by all, but feared by the powerful and the fortunate. She is said to be the daughter of Nox and Oceanus. She is drawn with wings, and a crown ; a javelin of ash in her right hand ; a glass containing Ethiopians in her left ; and riding upon a stag.

Explanation.—The fable receives this explanation. The word Nemesis manifestly signifies revenge, or retribution ; for the office of this goddess consisted in interposing, like the Roman tribunes, with an " I forbid it," in all courses of constant and perpetual felicity, so as not only to chastise haughtiness, but also to repay even innocent and moderate happiness with adversity ; as if it were decreed, that none of human race should be admitted to the banquet of the gods, but for sport. And, indeed, to read over that chapter of Pliny wherein he has collected the miseries and misfortunes of Augustus Cæsar, whom of all mankind one would judge most fortunate,—as he had a certain art of using and enjoying prosperity, with a mind no way tumid, light, effeminate, confused, or melancholic,—one cannot but think this a very great and powerful goddess, who could bring such a victim to her altar.

The parents of this goddess were Oceanus and Nox ; that is, the fluctuating change of things, and the obscure and secret divine decrees. The changes of things are aptly represented by the Ocean, on account of its perpetual ebbing and flowing ; and secret providence is justly expressed by Night. Even the heathens have observed this secret Nemesis of the night, or the difference betwixt divine and human judgment.

Wings are given to Nemesis, because of the sudden and unforeseen changes of things ; for, from the earliest account of time, it has been common for great and prudent men to fall by the dangers they most despised. Thus Cicero, when admonished by Brutus of the infidelity and rancor of Octavius, coolly wrote back, " I cannot, however, but be obliged to you, Brutus, as I ought, for informing me, though of such a trifle."

Nemesis also has her crown, by reason of the invidious and malignant nature of the vulgar, who generally rejoice, triumph, and crown her, at the fall of the fortunate and the powerful. And the javelin in her right hand, it has regard to those whom she has actually struck and transfixed. But whoever escapes her stroke, or feels not actual calamity or misfortune, she affrights with a black and dismal sight in her left hand ; for doubtless, mortals on the highest pinnacle of felicity have a prospect of death, diseases, calamities, perfidious friends, undermining enemies, reverses of fortune, etc., represented by the Ethiopians in her glass. Thus Virgil, with great elegance, describing the battle of Actium, says of Cleopatra, that, " she did not yet perceive the two asps behind her " ; but soon after, which way soever she turned, she saw whole troops of Ethiopians still before her.

Lastly, it is significantly added, that Nemesis rides upon a stag, which is a very long-lived creature ; for though perhaps some, by an untimely death in youth, may prevent or escape this goddess, yet they who enjoy a long flow of happiness and power, doubtless become subject to her at length, and are brought to yield.

XXIII.—ACHELOUS : OR BATTLE.

EXPLAINED OF WAR BY INVASION.

The ancients relate, that Hercules and Achelous being rivals in the courtship of Deianira, the matter was contested by single combat ; when Achelous having transformed himself, as he had power to do, into various shapes, by way of trial ; at length, in the form of a fierce wild bull, prepares himself for the fight ; but Hercules still retains his human shape, engages sharply with him, and in the issue broke off one of the bull's horns ; and now Achelous, in great pain and fright, to redeem his horn, presents Hercules with the cornucopia.

Explanation.—This fable relates to military expeditions and preparations ; for the preparation of war on the defensive side, here denoted by Achelous, appears in various shapes, whilst the invading side has but one simple form, consisting either in an army, or perhaps a fleet. But the country that expects the invasion is employed infinite ways, in fortifying towns, blockading passes, rivers, and ports, raising soldiers, disposing garrisons, building and breaking down bridges, procuring aids, securing provisions, arms, ammunition, etc. So that there appears a new face of things every day ; and at length, when the country is sufficiently fortified and prepared, it represents to the life the form and threats of a fierce fighting bull.

On the other side, the invader presses on to the fight, fearing to be distressed in an enemy's country. And if after the battle he remains master of the field, and has now broke, as it were, the horn of his enemy, the

besieged, of course, retire inglorious, affrighted, and
dismayed, to their stronghold, there endeavoring to
secure themselves, and repair their strength ; leaving,
at the same time, their country a prey to the conqueror,
which is well expressed by the Amalthean horn, or
cornucopia.

XXIV.—DIONYSUS : OR BACCHUS.
EXPLAINED OF THE PASSIONS.

The fable runs, that Semele, Jupiter's mistress,
having bound him by an inviolable oath to grant her
an unknown request, desired he would embrace her in
the same form and manner he used to embrace Juno ;
and the promise being irrevocable, she was burnt to
death with lightning in the performance. The embry
however, was sewed up, and carried in Jupiter's thigh
till the complete time of its birth ; but the burthen,
thus rendering the father lame, and causing him pain,
the child was thence called Dionysus. When born, he
was committed for some years, to be nursed by Proserpina ; and when grown up, appeared with so effeminate a face, that his sex seemed somewhat doubtful.
He also died, and was buried for a time, but afterwards
revived. When a youth, he first introduced the cultivation and dressing of vines, the method of preparing
wine, and taught the use thereof ; whence becoming
famous, he subdued the world, even to the utmost
bounds of the Indies. He rode in a chariot drawn by
tigers. There danced about him certain deformed
demons called Cobali, etc. The Muses also joined in
his train. He married Ariadne, who was deserted by
Theseus. The ivy was sacred to him. He was also
held the inventor and institutor of religious rites and
ceremonies, but such as were wild, frantic and full of

corruption and cruelty. He had also the power of
striking men with frenzies. Pentheus and Orpheus
were torn to pieces by the frantic women at his orgies ;
the first for climbing a tree to behold their outrageous
ceremonies, and the other for the music of his harp.
But the acts of this god are much entangled and confounded with those of Jupiter.

Explanation.—This fable seems to contain a little
system of morality, so that there is scarce any better
invention in all ethics. Under the history of Bacchus
is drawn the nature of unlawful desire or affection,
and disorder ; for the appetite and thirst of apparent
good is the mother of all unlawful desire, though ever
so destructive, and all unlawful desires are conceived
in unlawful wishes or requests, rashly indulged or
granted before they are well understood or considered,
and when the affection begins to grow warm, the
mother of it (the nature of good) is destroyed and
burnt up by the heat. And whilst an unlawful desire
lies in the embryo, or unripened in the mind, which
is its father, and here represented by Jupiter, it is
cherished and concealed, especially in the inferior part
of the mind, corresponding to the thigh of the body,
where pain twitches and depresses the mind so far as
to render its resolutions and actions imperfect and
lame. And even after this child of the mind is confirmed, and gains strength by consent and habit, and
comes forth into action, it must still be nursed by
Proserpina for a time ; that is, it skulks and hides its
head in a clandestine manner, as it were under ground,
till at length, when the checks of shame and fear are
removed, and the requisite boldness acquired, it either
assumes the pretext of some virtue, or openly despises
infamy. And it is justly observed, that every vehement
passion appears of a doubtful sex, as having the strength
of a man at first, but at last the impotence of a woman.

It is also excellently added, that Bacchus died and rose again ; for the affections sometimes seem to die and be no more ; but there is no trusting them, even though they were buried, being always apt and ready to rise again whenever the occasion or object offers.

That Bacchus should be the inventor of wine carries a fine allegory with it ; for every affection is cunning and subtile in discovering a proper manner to nourish and feed it ; and of all things known to mortals, wine is the most powerful and effectual for exciting and inflaming passions of all kinds, being indeed like a common fuel to all.

It is again with great elegance observed of Bacchus, that he subdued provinces, and undertook endless expeditions, for the affections never rest satisfied with what they enjoy, but with an endless and insatiable appetite, thirst after something further. And tigers are prettily feigned to draw the chariot ; for as soon as any affection shall, from going on foot, be advanced to ride, it triumphs over reason, and exerts its cruelty, fierceness, and strength against all that oppose it.

It is also humorously imagined, that ridiculous demons dance and frisk about this chariot ; for every passion produces indecent, disorderly, interchangeable, · deformed motions in the eyes, countenance, and gesture, so that the person under the impulse, whether of anger, insult, love, etc., though to himself, he may seen grand, lofty, or obliging, yet in the eyes of others appears mean, contemptible, or ridiculous.

The Muses also are found in the train of Bacchus, for there is scarce any passion without its art, science, or doctrine to court and flatter it ; but in this respect the indulgence of men of genius has greatly detracted from the majesty of the Muses, who ought to be the leaders and conductors of human life, and not the handmaids of the passions.

The allegory of Bacchus falling in love with a cast mistress, is extremely noble ; for it is certain that the affections always court and covet what has been rejected upon experience. And all those who by serving and indulging their passions immensely raise the value of enjoyment, should know, that whatever they covet and pursue, whether riches, pleasure, glory, learning, or anything else, they only pursue those things that have been forsaken and cast off with contempt by great numbers in all ages, after possession and experience.

Nor is it without a mystery that the ivy was sacred to Bacchus, and this for two reasons : first, because ivy is an evergreen, or flourishes in the winter; and secondly, because it winds and creeps about so many things, as trees, walls, and buildings, and raises itself above them. As to the first, every passion grows fresh, strong, and vigorous by opposition and prohibition, as it were by a kind of contrast or antiperistasis, like the ivy in the winter. And for the second, the predominant passion of the mind throws itself, like the ivy, round all human actions, entwines all our resolutions, and perpetually adheres to, and mixes itself among, or even overtops them.

And no wonder that superstitious rites and cere- monies are attributed to Bacchus, when almost every ungovernable passion grows wanton and luxuriant in corrupt religions ; nor again, that fury and frenzy should be sent and dealt out by him, because every passion is a short frenzy, and if it be vehement, lasting, and take deep root, it terminates in madness. And hence the allegory of Pentheus and Orpheus being torn to pieces is evident ; for every headstrong passion is extremely bitter, severe, inveterate, and revengeful upon all curious inquiry, wholesome admonition, free counsel and persuasion.

Lastly, the confusion between the persons of Jupiter

and Bacchus will justly admit of an allegory, because noble and meritorious actions may sometimes proceed from virtue, sound reason, and magnanimity, and sometimes again from a concealed passion and secret desire of ill, however they may be extolled and praised, insomuch that it is not easy to distinguish betwixt the acts of Bacchus and the acts of Jupiter.

XXV.—ATALANTA AND HIPPOMENES : OR GAIN.

EXPLAINED OF THE CONTEST BETWIXT ART AND NATURE.

Atalanta, who was exceeding fleet, contended with Hippomenes in the course, on condition that if Hippomenes won, he should espouse her, or forfeit his life if he lost. The match was very unequal, for Atalanta had conquered numbers, to their destruction. Hippomenes, therefore, had recourse to stratagem. He procured three golden apples, and purposely carried them with him : they started ; Atalanta outstripped him soon ; then Hippomenes bowled one of his apples before her, across the course, in order not only to make her stoop, but to draw her out of the path. She, prompted by female curiosity, and the beauty of the golden fruit, starts from the course to take up the apple. Hippomenes, in the mean time, holds on his way, and steps before her ; but she, by her natural swiftness, soon fetches up her lost ground, and leaves him again behind. Hippomenes, however, by rightly timing his second and third throw, at length won the race, not by his swiftness, but his cunning.

Explanation.—This fable seems to contain a noble allegory of the contest betwixt art and nature. For art here denoted by Atalanta, is much swifter, or more expeditious in its operations than nature, when all obstacles and impediments are removed, and sooner arrives at its end. This appears almost in every instance. Thus fruit comes slowly from the kernel, but soon by inoculation or incision ; clay, left to itself, is a long time in acquiring a stony hardness, but is presently burnt by fire into brick. So again in human life, nature is a long while in alleviating and abolishing the remembrance of pain, and assuaging the troubles of the mind ; but moral philosophy, which is the art of living, performs it presently. Yet this prerogative and singular efficacy of art is stopped and retarded to the infinite detriment of human life, by certain golden apples ; for there is no one science or art that constantly holds on its true and proper course to the end, but they are all continually stopping short, forsaking the track, and turning aside to profit and convenience, exactly like Atalanta. Whence it is no wonder that art gets not the victory over nature, nor, according to the condition of the contest, brings her under subjection ; but, on the contrary, remains subject to her, as a wife to a husband.

XXVI.—PROMETHEUS : OR THE STATE OF MAN.

EXPLAINED OF AN OVER-RULING PROVIDENCE, AND OF HUMAN NATURE.

The ancients relate that man was the work of Prometheus, and formed of clay ; only the artificer mixed in with the mass, particles taken from different animals. And being desirous to improve his workmanship, and endow, as well as create, the human race, he stole up to heaven with a bundle of birch-rods, and kindling them at the chariot of the Sun, thence brought down fire to the earth for the service of men.

They add, that for this meritorious act Prometheus was repayed with ingratitude by mankind, so that, forming a conspiracy, they arraigned both him and his invention before Jupiter. But the matter was otherwise received than they imagined ; for the accusation proved extremely grateful to Jupiter and the gods, insomuch that, delighted with the action, they not only indulged mankind the use of fire, but moreover conferred upon them a most acceptable and desirable present, namely, perpetual youth.

But men, foolishly overjoyed hereat, laid this present of the gods upon an ass, who, in returning back with it, being extremely thirsty, strayed to a fountain. The serpent, who was guardian thereof, would not suffer him to drink, but upon condition of receiving the burden he carried, whatever it should be. The silly ass complied, and thus the perpetual renewal of youth was, for a drop of water, transferred from men to the race of serpents.

Prometheus, not desisting from his unwarrantable practices, though now reconciled to mankind, after they were thus tricked of their present, but still continuing inveterate against Jupiter, had the boldness to attempt deceit, even in a sacrifice, and is said to have once offered up two bulls to Jupiter, but so as in the hide of one of them to wrap all the flesh and fat of both, and stuffing out the other hide only with the bones ; then in a religious and devout manner, gave Jupiter his choice of the two. Jupiter, detesting this sly fraud and hypocrisy, but having thus an opportunity of punishing the offender, purposely chose the mock bull.

And now giving way to revenge, but finding he could not chastise the insolence of Prometheus without afflicting the human race (in the production whereof Prometheus had strangely and insufferably prided him-

self), he commanded Vulcan to form a beautiful and
graceful woman, to whom every god presented a certain
gift, whence she was called Pandora. They put into
her hands an elegant box, containing all sorts of
miseries and misfortunes ; but Hope was placed at the
bottom of it. With this box she first goes to Prometheus, to try if she could prevail upon him to receive
and open it; but he, being upon his guard, warily
refused the offer. Upon this refusal, she comes to his
brother Epimetheus, a man of a very different temper,
who rashly and inconsiderately opens the box. When
finding all kinds of miseries and misfortunes issued
out of it, he grew wise too late, and with great hurry
and struggle endeavored to clap the cover on again ;
but with all his endeavor could scarce keep in Hope,
which lay at the bottom.

Lastly, Jupiter arraigned Prometheus of many
heinous crimes : as that he formerly stole fire from
heaven ; that he contemptuously and deceitfully
mocked him by a sacrifice of bones ; that he despised
his present, adding withal a new crime, that he
attempted to ravish Pallas : for all which, he was
sentenced to be bound in chains, and doomed to perpetual torments. Accordingly, by Jupiter's command,
he was brought to Mount Caucasus, and there fastened
to a pillar, so firmly that he could no way stir. A
vulture or eagle stood by him, which in the daytime
gnawed and consumed his liver ; but in the night the
wasted parts were supplied again ; whence matter for
his pain was never wanting.

They relate, however, that his punishment had an
end ; for Hercules sailing the ocean, in a cup, or
pitcher, presented him by the Sun, came at length to
Caucasus, shot the eagle with his arrows, and set
Prometheus free. In certain nations, also, there were
instituted particular games of the torch, to the honor

of Prometheus, in which they who ran for the prize carried lighted torches ; and as any one of these torches happened to go out, the bearer withdrew himself, and gave way to the next ; and that person was allowed to win the prize who first brought in his lighted torch to the goal.

Explanation.—This fable contains and enforces many just and serious considerations ; some whereof have been long since well observed, but some again remain perfectly untouched. Prometheus clearly and expressly signifies Providence ; for of all things in nature, the formation and endowment of man was singled out by the ancients, and esteemed the peculiar work of Providence. The reason hereof seems, 1. That the nature of man includes a mind and understanding, which is the seat of Providence. 2. That it is harsh and incredible to suppose reason and mind should be raised, and drawn out of senseless and irrational principles ; whence it becomes almost inevitable, that providence is implanted in the human mind in conformity with, and by the direction and the design of the greater over-ruling Providence. But, 3. The principal cause is this : that man seems to be the thing in which the whole world centres, with respect to final causes ; so that if he were away, all other things would stray and fluctuate, without end or intention, or become perfectly disjointed, and out of frame ; for all things are made subservient to man, and he receives use and benefit from them all. Thus the revolutions, places, and periods, of the celestial bodies, serve him for distinguishing times and seasons, and for dividing the world into different regions ; the meteors afford him prognostications of the weather ; the winds sail our ships, drive our mills, and move our machines ; and the vegetables and animals of all kinds either afford us matter for houses and habitations, clothing, food,

physic, or tend to ease, or delight, to support, or refresh
us : so that everything in nature seems not made for
itself, but for man.

And it is not without reason added, that the mass of
matter whereof man was formed, should be mixed up
with particles taken from different animals, and
wrought in with the clay, because it is certain, that of
all the things in the universe, man is the most com-
pounded and recompounded body ; so that the ancients
not improperly styled him a Microcosm, or little world
within himself. For although the chemists have
absurdly, and too literally, wrested and perverted the
elegance of the term microcosm, whilst they pretend
to find all kind of mineral and vegetable matters, or
something corresponding to them, in man, yet it
remains firm and unshaken, that the human body is of
all substances the most mixed and organical ; whence
it has surprising powers and faculties : for the powers
of simple bodies are but few, though certain and quick;
as being little broken, or weakened, and not counter-
balanced by mixture : but excellence and quantity of
energy reside in mixture and composition.

Man, however, in his first origin, seems to be a
defenceless naked creature, slow in assisting himself,
and standing in need of numerous things. Prometheus,
therefore, hastened to the invention of fire, which
supplies and administers to nearly all human uses and
necessities, insomuch that, if the soul may be called
the form of forms, if the hand may be called the
instrument of instruments, fire may as properly be
called the assistant of assistants, or helper of helps; for
hence proceed numberless operations, hence all the
mechanic arts, and hence infinite assistances are
afforded to the sciences themselves.

The manner wherein Prometheus stole this fire is
properly described from the nature of the thing ; he

being said to have done it by applying a rod of birch
to the chariot of the Sun : for birch is used in striking
and beating, which clearly denotes the generation of
fire to be from the violent percussions and collisions of
bodies ; whereby the matters struck are subtilised,
rarefied, put into motion, and so prepared to receive
the heat of the celestial bodies ; whence they, in a
clandestine and secret manner, collect and snatch fire,
as it were by stealth, from the chariot of the Sun.

The next is a remarkable part of the fable, which
represents that men, instead of gratitude and thanks,
fell into indignation and expostulation, accusing both
Prometheus and his fire to Jupiter,—and yet the accusation proved highly pleasing to Jupiter ; so that he, for
this reason, crowned these benefits of mankind with a -
new bounty. Here it may seem strange that the sin of
ingratitude to a creator and benefactor, a sin so heinous
as to include almost all others, should meet with appro-
bation and reward. But the allegory has another view,
and denotes, that the accusation and arraignment, both
of human nature and human art among mankind,
proceeds from a most noble and laudable temper of the
mind, and tends to a very good purpose ; whereas the
contrary temper is odious to the gods, and unbeneficial
in itself. For they who break into extravagant praises
of human nature and the arts in vogue, and who lay
themselves out in admiring the things they already
possess, and will needs have the sciences cultivated
among them, to be thought absolutely perfect and
complete, in the first place, show little regard to
the divine nature, whilst they extol their own
inventions almost as high as his perfection. In the
next place, men of this temper are unserviceable and
prejudicial in life, whilst they imagine themselves
already got to the top of things, and there rest, without
farther inquiry. On the contrary, they who arraign

E

and accuse both nature and art, and are always full of complaints against them, not only preserve a more just and modest sense of mind, but are also perpetually stirred up to fresh industry and new discoveries. Is not, then, the ignorance and fatality of mankind to be extremely pitied, whilst they remain slaves to the arrogance of a few of their own fellows, and are dotingly fond of that scrap of Grecian knowledge, the Peripatetic philosophy ; and this to such a degree, as not only to think all accusation or arraignment thereof useless, but even hold it suspect and dangerous ? Certainly the procedure of Empedocles, though furious— but especially that of Democritus (who with great modesty complained that all things were abstruse ; that we know nothing ; that truth lies hid in deep pits ; that falsehood is strangely joined and twisted along with truth, etc.)—is to be preferred before the confident, assuming, and dogmatical school of Aristotle. Mankind are, therefore, to be admonished, that the arraignment of nature and of art is pleasing to the gods ; and that a sharp and vehement accusation of Prometheus, though a creator, a founder, and a master, obtained new blessings and presents from the divine bounty, and proved more sound and serviceable than a diffusive harangue of praise and gratulation. And let men be assured that the fond opinion that they have already acquired enough, is a principal reason why they have acquired so little.

That the perpetual flower of youth should be the present which mankind received as a reward for their accusation, carries this moral : that the ancients seem not to have despaired of discovering methods, and remedies, for retarding old age, and prolonging the period of human life, but rather reckoned it among those things which, through sloth and want of diligent inquiry, perish and come to nothing, after having been once undertaken, than among such as are absolutely impossible, or placed beyond the reach of the human power. For they signify and intimate from the true use of fire, and the just and strenuous accusation and conviction of the errors of art, that the divine bounty is not wanting to men in such kind of presents, but that men indeed are wanting to themselves, and lay such an inestimable gift upon the back of a slow-paced ass ; that is, upon the back of the heavy, dull, lingering thing, experience; from whose sluggish and tortoise-pace proceeds that ancient complaint of the shortness of life, and the slow advancement of arts. And certainly it may well seem, that the two faculties of reasoning and experience are not hitherto properly joined and coupled together, but to be still new gifts of the gods, separately laid, the one upon the back of a light bird, or abstract philosophy, and the other upon an ass, or slow-paced practice and trial. And yet good hopes might be conceived of this ass, if it were not for his thirst and the accidents of the way. For we judge, that if any one would constantly proceed, by a certain law and method, in the road of experience, and not by the way thirst after such experiments as make for profit or ostentation, nor exchange his burden, or quit the original design for the sake of these, he might be a useful bearer of a new and accumulated divine bounty to mankind.

That this gift of perpetual youth should pass from men to serpents, seems added by way of ornament, and illustration to the fable ; perhaps intimating, at the same time, the shame it is for men, that they, with their fire, and numerous arts, cannot procure to them-selves those things which nature has bestowed upon many other creatures.

The sudden reconciliation of Prometheus to man-kind, after being disappointed of their hopes, contains

a prudent and useful admonition. It points out the
levity and temerity of men in new experiments, when,
not presently succeeding, or answering to expectation,
they precipitantly quit their new undertakings, hurry
back to their old ones, and grow reconciled thereto.

After the fable has described the state of man, with
regard to arts and intellectual matters, it passes on to
religion ; for after the inventing and settling of arts,
follows the establishment of divine worship, which
hypocrisy presently enters into and corrupts. So that
by the two sacrifices we have elegantly painted the
person of a man truly religious, and of an hypocrite.
One of these sacrifices contained the fat, or the portion
of God, used for burning and incensing ; thereby
denoting affection and zeal, offered up to his glory. It
likewise contained the bowels, which are expressive of
charity, along with the good and useful flesh. But the
other contained nothing more than dry bones, which
nevertheless stuffed out the hide, so as to make it
resemble a fair, beautiful, and magnificent sacrifice ;
hereby finely denoting the external and empty rites
and barren ceremonies, wherewith men burden and
stuff out the divine worship,—things rather intended
for show and ostentation than conducing to piety.
Nor are mankind simply content with this mock-
worship of God, but also impose and father it upon
him, as if he had chosen and ordained it. Certainly
the prophet, in the person of God, has a fine expostulation, as to this matter of choice :—" Is this the
fasting which I have chosen, that a man should afflict
his soul for a day, and bow down his head like
bulrush ?"

After thus touching the state of religion, the fable
next turns to manners, and the conditions of human
life. And though it be a very common, yet is it a just
interpretation, that Pandora denotes the pleasures and

licentiousness which the cultivation and luxury of the arts of civil life introduce, as it were, by the instrumental efficacy of fire ; whence the works of the voluptuary arts are properly attributed to Vulcan, the God of Fire. And hence infinite miseries and calamities have proceeded to the minds, the bodies, and the fortunes of men, together with a late repentance ; and this not only in each man's particular, but also in kingdoms and states ; for wars, and tumults, and tyrannies, have all arisen from this same fountain, or box of Pandora.

It is worth observing, how beautifully and elegantly the fable has drawn two reigning characters in human life, and given two examples, or tablatures of them, under the persons of Prometheus and Epimetheus. The followers of Epimetheus are improvident, see not far before them, and prefer such things as are agreeable for the present ; whence they are oppressed with numerous straits, difficulties, and calamities, with which they almost continually struggle ; but in the meantime gratify their own temper, and, for want of a better knowledge of things, feed their minds with many vain hopes ; and as with so many pleasing dreams, delight themselves, and sweeten the miseries of life.

But the followers of Prometheus are the prudent, wary men, that look into futurity, and cautiously guard against, prevent, and undermine many calamities and misfortunes. But this watchful, provident temper, is attended with a deprivation of numerous pleasures, and the loss of various delights, whilst such men debar themselves the use even of innocent things, and what is still worse, rack and torture themselves with cares, fears, and disquiets ; being bound fast to the pillar of necessity. and tormented with numberless thoughts (which for their swiftness are well compared to an eagle), that continually wound, tear, and gnaw their liver or mind, unless, perhaps, they find some small remission by intervals, or as it were at nights; but then new anxieties, dreads, and fears, soon return again, as it were in the morning. And, therefore, very few men, of either temper, have secured to themselves the advantages of providence, and kept clear of disquiets, troubles, and misfortunes.

Nor indeed can any man obtain this end without the assistance of Hercules; that is, of such fortitude and constancy of mind as stands prepared against every event, and remains indifferent to every change; looking forward without being daunted, enjoying the good without disdain, and enduring the bad without impatience. And it must be observed, that even Prometheus had not the power to free himself, but owed his deliverance to another; for no natural inbred force and fortitude could prove equal to such a task. The power of releasing him came from the utmost confines of the ocean, and from the sun; that is, from Apollo, or knowledge; and again, from a due consideration of the uncertainty, instability, and fluctuating state of human life, which is aptly represented by sailing the ocean. Accordingly, Virgil has prudently joined these two together, accounting him happy who knows the causes of things, and has conquered all his fears, apprehensions, and superstitions.

It is added, with great elegance, for supporting and confirming the human mind, that the great hero who thus delivered him sailed the ocean in a cup, or pitcher, to prevent fear, or complaint; as if, through the narrowness of our nature, or a too great fragility thereof, we were absolutely incapable of that fortitude and constancy to which Seneca finely alludes, when he says, " It is a noble thing, at once to participate in the frailty of man and the security of a god."

We have hitherto, that we might not break the connection of things, designedly omitted the last crime, of Prometheus—that of attempting the chastity of Minerva—which heinous offence it doubtless was, that caused the punishment of having his liver gnawed by the vulture. The meaning seems to be this,—that when men are puffed up with arts and knowledge, they often try to subdue even the divine wisdom and bring it under the dominion of sense and reason, whence inevitably follows a perpetual and restless rending and tearing of the mind. A sober and humble distinction must, therefore, be made betwixt divine and human things, and betwixt the oracles of sense and faith, unless mankind had rather choose an heretical religion, and a fictitious and romantic philosophy.

The last particular in the fable is the Games of the Torch, instituted to Prometheus, which again relates to arts and sciences, as well as the invention of fire, for the commemoration and celebration whereof these games were held. And here we have an extremely prudent admonition, directing us to expect the perfection of the sciences from succession, and not from the swiftness and abilities of any single person ; for he who is fleetest and strongest in the course may perhaps be less fit to keep his torch alight, since there is danger of its going out from too rapid as well as from too slow a motion. But this kind of contest, with the torch, seems to have been long dropped and neglected ; the sciences appearing to have flourished principally in their first authors, as Aristotle, Galen, Euclid, Ptolemy, etc. ; whilst their successors have done very little, or scarce made any attempts. But it were highly to be wished that these games might be renewed, to the honor of Prometheus, or human nature, and that they might excite contest, emulation, and laudable endeavors, and the design meet with such success as not to hang tottering, tremulous, and hazarded, upon the torch of any single person. Mankind, therefore, should be admonished to rouse themselves, and try and exert their own strength and chance, and not place all their dependence upon a few men, whose abilities and capacities, perhaps, are not greater than their own.

These are the particulars which appear to us shadowed out by this trite and vulgar fable, though without denying that there may be contained in it several intimations that have a surprising correspondence with the Christian mysteries. In particular, the voyage of Hercules, made in a pitcher, to release Prometheus, bears an allusion to the word of God, coming in the frail vessel of the flesh to redeem mankind. But we indulge ourselves no such liberties as these, for fear of using strange fire at the altar of the Lord.

XXVII.—ICARUS AND SCYLLA AND CHARYBDIS : OR THE MIDDLE WAY.

EXPLAINED OF MEDIOCRITY IN NATURAL AND MORAL PHILOSOPHY.

Mediocrity, or the holding a middle course, has been highly extolled in morality, but little in matters of science, though no less useful and proper here ; whilst in politics it is held suspected, and ought to be employed with judgment. The ancients described mediocrity in manners by the course prescribed to Icarus ; and in matters of the understanding by the steering betwixt Scylla and Charybdis, on account of the great difficulty and danger in passing those straits.

Icarus, being to fly across the sea, was ordered by his father neither to soar too high nor fly too low, for, as his wings were fastened together with wax, there was danger of its melting by the sun's heat in too high a flight, and of its becoming less tenacious by the moisture if he kept too near the vapor of the sea. But he, with a juvenile confidence, soared aloft, and fell down headlong.

Explanation.—The fable is vulgar, and easily interpreted; for the path of virtue lies straight between excess on the one side, and defect on the other. And no wander that excess should prove the bane of Icarus, exulting in juvenile strength and vigor; for excess is the natural vice of youth, as defect is that of old age; and if a man must perish by either, Icarus chose the better of the two; for all defects are justly esteemed more depraved than excesses. There is some magnanimity in excess, that, like a bird, claims kindred with the heavens; but defect is a reptile, that basely crawls upon the earth. It was excellently said by Heraclitus, "A dry light makes the best soul"; for if the soul contracts moisture from the earth, it perfectly degenerates and sinks. On the other hand, moderation must be observed, to prevent this fine light from burning, by its too great subtilty and dryness. But these observations are common.

In matters of the understanding, it requires great skill and a particular felicity to steer clear of Scylla and Charybdis. If the ship strikes upon Scylla, it is dashed in pieces against the rocks; if upon Charybdis, it is swallowed outright. This allegory is pregnant with matter; but we shall only observe that the force of it lies here, that a mean be observed in every doctrine and science, and in the rules and axioms thereof, between the rocks of distinctions and the whirlpools of universalities; for these two are the bane and shipwreck of fine geniuses and arts.

XXVIII.—SPHINX : OR SCIENCE.

EXPLAINED OF THE SCIENCES.

They relate that Sphinx was a monster, variously formed, having the face and voice of a virgin, the wings of a bird, and the talons of a griffin. She resided on the top of a mountain, near the city Thebes, and also beset the highways. Her manner was to lie in ambush and seize the travellers, and having them in her power, to propose to them certain dark and perplexed riddles, which it was thought she received from the Muses, and if her wretched captives could not solve and interpret these riddles, she with great cruelty fell upon them, in their hesitation and confusion, and tore them to pieces. This plague having reigned a long time, the Thebans at length offered their kingdom to the man who could interpret her riddles, there being no other way to subdue her. Œdipus, a penetrating and prudent man, though lame in his feet, excited by so great a reward, accepted the condition, and with a good assurance of mind, cheerfully presented himself before the monster, who directly asked him, " What creature that was, which being born four-footed, afterwards became two-footed, then three-footed, and lastly four-footed again ?" Œdipus, with presence of mind, replied it was man, who, upon his first birth and infant state, crawled upon all fours in endeavoring to walk ; but not long after went upright upon his two natural feet ; again, in old age walked three-footed, with a stick ; and at last, growing decrepit, lay four-footed confined to his bed ; and having by this exact solution obtained the victory, he slew the monster, and, laying the carcass upon an ass, led her away in triumph ; and upon this he was, according to the agreement, made king of Thebes.

Explanation.—This is an elegant, instructive fable, and seems invented to represent science, especially as joined with practice. For science may, without absurdity, be called a monster, being strangely gazed at and admired by the ignorant and unskilful. Her figure and form is various, by reason of the vast variety of subjects that science considers ; her voice and countenance are represented female, by reason of her gay appearance and volubility of speech ; wings are added, because the sciences and their inventions run and fly about in a moment, for knowledge, like light communicated from one torch to another, is presently caught and copiously diffused ; sharp and hooked talons are elegantly attributed to her, because the axioms and arguments of science enter the mind, lay hold of it, fix it down, and keep it from moving or slipping away. This the sacred philosopher observed, when he said, " The words of the wise are like goads or nails driven far in." Again, all science seems placed on high, as it were on the tops of mountains that are hard to climb ; for science is justly imagined a sublime and lofty thing, looking down upon ignorance from an eminence, and at the same time taking an extensive view on all sides, as is usual on the tops of mountains. Science is said to beset the highways, because through all the journey and peregrination of human life there is matter and occasion offered of contemplation.

Sphinx is said to propose various difficult questions and riddles to men, which she received from the Muses ; and these questions, so long as they remain with the Muses, may very well be unaccompanied with severity, for while there is no other end of contemplation and inquiry but that of knowledge alone, the understanding is not opposed, or driven to straits and difficulties, but expatiates and ranges at large, and even receives a degree of pleasure from doubt and variety; but after the Muses have given over their riddles to Sphinx, that is, to practice, which urges and impels to action, choice, and determination, then it is that they become torturing, severe, and trying, and, unless solved and interpreted, strangely perplex and harass the human mind, rend it every way, and perfectly tear it to pieces. All the riddles of Sphinx, therefore, have two conditions annexed, namely, dilaceration to those who do not solve them, and empire to those that do. For he who understands the thing proposed obtains his end, and every artificer rules over his work.

Sphinx has no more than two kinds of riddles, one relating to the nature of things, the other to the nature of man; and correspondent to these, the prizes of the solution are two kinds of empire,—the empire over nature, and the empire over man. For the true and ultimate end of natural philosophy is dominion over natural things, natural bodies, remedies, machines, and numberless other particulars, though the schools, contended with what spontaneously offers, and swollen with their own discourses, neglect, and in a manner despise, both things and works.

But the riddle proposed to Œdipus, the solution whereof acquired him the Theban kingdon, regarded the nature of man; for he who has throughly looked into and examined human nature, may in a manner command his own fortune, and seems born to acquire dominion and rule. Accordingly, Virgil properly makes the arts of government to be the arts of the Romans. It was, therefore extremely apposite in Augustus Cæsar to use the image of Sphinx in his signet, whether this happened by accident or by design; for he of all men was deeply versed in politics, and through the course of his life very happily solved abundance of new riddles with regard to the nature of man ; and unless he had done this with great dexterity and ready address, he would frequently have been involved in imminent danger, if not destruction.

It is with the utmost elegance added in the fable, that when Sphinx was conquered, her carcass was laid upon an ass ; for there is nothing so subtile and abstruse, but after being once made plain, intelligible, and common, it may be received by the slowest capacity.

We must not omit that Sphinx was conquered by a lame man, and impotent in his feet : for men usually make too much haste to the solution of Sphinx's riddles; whence it happens, that she prevailing, their minds are rather racked and torn by disputes, than invested with command by works and effects.

XXIX.—PROSERPINE : OR SPIRIT.

EXPLAINED OF THE SPIRIT INCLUDED IN NATURAL BODIES.

They tell us, Pluto having, upon that memorable division of empire among the gods, received the infernal regions for his share, despaired of winning any one of the goddesses in marriage by an obsequious courtship, and therefore through necessity resolved upon a rape. Having watched his opportunity, he suddenly seized upon Proserpine, a most beautiful virgin, the daughter of Ceres, as she was gathering narcissus flowers in the meads of Sicily, and hurrying her to his chariot, carried her with him to the subterraneal regions, where she was treated with the highest reverence, and styled the Lady of Dis. But Ceres missing her only daughter, whom she extremely loved, grew pensive and anxious beyond measure, and taking a lighted torch in her hand, wandered the world over in quest of her daughter,—but all to no purpose, till, suspecting she might be carried to the infernal regions, she, with great lamentation and abundance of tears, importuned Jupiter to restore her; and with much ado prevailed so far as to recover and bring her away, if she had tasted nothing there. This proved a hard condition upon the mother, for Proserpine was found to have eaten three kernels of a pomegranate. Ceres, however, desisted not, but fell to her entreaties and lamentations afresh, insomuch that at last it was indulged her that Proserpine should divide the year betwixt her husband and her mother, and live six months with the one and as many with the other. After this, Theseus, and Perithous, with uncommon audacity, attempted to force Proserpine away from Pluto's bed, but happening to grow tired in their journey, and resting themselves upon a stone in the realms below, they could never rise from it again, but remain sitting there for ever. Proserpine, therefore, still continued queen of the lower regions, in honor of whom there was also added this grand privilege, that though it had never been permitted any one to return after having once descended thither, a particular exception was made, that he who brought a golden bough as a present to Proserpine, might on that condition descend and return. This was an only bough that grew in a large dark grove, not from a tree of its own, but like the mistletoe, from another, and when plucked away a fresh one always shot out in its stead.

Explanation.—This fable seems to regard natural philosophy, and searches deep into that rich and fruitful virtue and supply in subterraneous bodies, from whence all the things upon the earth's surface spring, and into which they again relapse and return. By Proserpine the ancients denoted that ethereal spirit shut up and detained within the earth, here represented by Pluto,—the spirit being separated from the superior globe, according to the expression of the poet. This spirit is conceived as ravished, or snatched up by the earth, because it can no way be detained, when it has time and opportunity to fly off, but is only wrought together and fixed by sudden intermixture and comminution, in the same manner as if one should endeavor to mix air with water, which cannot otherwise be done than by a quick and rapid agitation, that joins them together in froth whilst the air is thus caught up by the water. And it is elegantly added, that Proserpine was ravished whilst she gathered narcissus flowers, which have their name from numbedness or stupefaction ; for the spirit we speak of is in the fittest disposition to be embraced by terrestrial matter when it begins to coagulate, or grow torpid as it were.

It is an honor justly attributed to Proserpine, and not to any other wife of the gods, that of being the lady or mistress of her husband, because this spirit performs all its operations in the subterraneal regions, whilst Pluto, or the earth, remains stupid, or as it were ignorant of them.

The æther, or the efficacy of the heavenly bodies, denoted by Ceres, endeavors with infinite diligence to force out this spirit, and restore it to its pristine state. And by the torch in the hand of Ceres, or the æther, is doubtless meant the sun, which disperses light over the whole globe of the earth, and if the thing were possible, must have the greatest share in recovering Proserpine, or reinstating the subterraneal spirit. Yet Proserpine still continues and dwells below, after the manner excellently described in the condition betwixt Jupiter and Ceres. For first, it is certain that there are two ways of detaining the spirit, in solid and terrestrial matter,—the one by condensation or obstruction, which is mere violence and imprisonment ; the other by administering a proper aliment, which is spontaneous and free. For after the included spirit begins to feed and nourish itself, it is not in a hurry to fly off, but remains, as it were, fixed in its own earth. And this is the moral of Proserpine's tasting the pomegranate ; and were it not for this, she must long ago have been carried up by Ceres, who with her torch wandered the world over, and so the earth have been left without its spirit. For though the spirit in metals and minerals may perhaps be, after a particular manner, wrought in by the solidity of the mass, yet the spirit of vegetables and animals has open passages to escape at, unless it be willingly detained, in the way of sipping and tasting them.

The second article of agreement, that of Proserpine's remaining six months with her mother and six with her husband, is an elegant description of the division of the year ; for the spirit diffused through the earth lives above-ground in the vegetable during the summer months, but in the winter returns under-ground again.

The attempts of Theseus and Perithous to bring Proserpine away, denotes that the more subtile spirits, which descend in many bodies to the earth, may frequently be unable to drink in, unite with themselves, and carry off the subterraneous spirit but on the contrary be coagulated by it, and rise no more, so as to increase the inhabitants and add to the dominion of Proserpine.

The alchemists will be apt to fall in with our interpretation of the golden bough, whether we will or no, because they promise golden mountains, and the restoration of natural bodies from their stone, as from the gates of Pluto ; but we are well assured that their theory has no just foundation, and suspect they have no very encouraging or practical proofs of its soundness. Leaving, therefore, their conceits to themselves, we shall freely declare our own sentiments upon this last part of the fable. We are certain, from numerous figures and expressions of the ancients, that they judged the conservation, and in some degree the renovation, of natural bodies to be no desperate or impossible thing, but rather abstruse and out of the common road than wholly impracticable. And this seems to be their opinion in the present case, as they have placed this bough among an infinite number of shrubs, in a spacious and thick wood. They supposed it of gold, because gold is the emblem of duration. They feigned it adventitious, not native, because such an effect is to be expected from art, and not from any medicine or any simple or mere natural way of working.

XXX.—METIS: OR COUNSEL.

EXPLAINED OF PRINCES AND THEIR COUNCIL.

The ancient poets relate that Jupiter took Metis to wife, whose name plainly denotes counsel, and that he, perceiving she was pregnant by him, would by no means wait the time of her delivery, but directly devoured her; whence himself also became pregnant, and was delivered in a wonderful manner; for he from his head or brain brought forth Pallas armed.

Explanation.—This fable, which in its literal sense appears monstrously absurd, seems to contain a state secret, and shows with what art kings usually carry themselves towards their council, in order to preserve their own authority and majesty not only inviolate, but so as to have it magnified and heightened among the people. For kings commonly link themselves, as it were, in a nuptial bond to their council, and deliberate and communicate with them after a prudent and laudable custom upon matters of the greatest importance, at the same time justly conceiving this no diminution of their majesty ; but when the matter once ripens to a decree or order, which is a kind of birth, the king then suffers the council to go on no further, lest the act should seem to depend upon their pleasure. Now, therefore, the king usually assumes to himself whatever was wrought, elaborated, or formed, as it were, in the womb of the council (unless it be a matter of an invidious nature, which he is sure to put from him), so that the decree and the execution shall seem to flow from himself. And as this decree or execution proceeds with prudence and power, so as to imply necessity, it is elegantly wrapt up under the figure of Pallas armed.

Nor are kings content to have this seem the effect of their own authority, free will, and uncontrollable choice, unless they also take the whole honor to themselves, and make the people imagine that all good and wholesome decrees proceed entirely from their own head, that is, their own sole prudence and judgment.

XXXI.—THE SIRENS : OR PLEASURES.
EXPLAINED OF MEN'S PASSION FOR PLEASURES.

Introduction.—The fable of the Sirens is, in a vulgar sense, justly enough explained of the pernicious incentives to pleasure ; but the ancient mythology seems to us like a vintage ill-pressed and trod; for though something has been drawn from it, yet all the more excellent parts remain behind in the grapes that are untouched.

Fable.—The Sirens are said to be the daughters of Achelous and Terpsichore, one of the Muses. In their early days they had wings, but lost them upon being conquered by the Muses, with whom they rashly contended ; and with the feathers of these wings the Muses made themselves crowns, so that from this time the Muses wore wings on their heads, excepting only the mother to the Sirens.

These Sirens resided in certain pleasant islands, and when, from their watch-tower, they saw any ship approaching, they first detained the sailors by their music, then, enticing them to shore, destroyed them.

Their singing was not of one and the same kind, but they adapted their tunes exactly to the nature of each person, in order to captivate and secure him. And so destructive had they been, that these islands of the Sirens appeared, to a very great distance, white with the bones of their unburied captives.

Two different remedies were invented to protect persons against them, the one by Ulysses, the other by Orpheus. Ulysses commanded his associates to stop their ears close with wax ; and he, determining to make the trial, and yet avoid the danger, ordered himself to be tied fast to a mast of the ship, giving strict charge not to be unbound, even though himself should entreat it ; but Orpheus, without any binding at all, escaped the danger, by loudly chanting to his harp the praises of the gods, whereby he drowned the voices of the Sirens.

Explanation.—This fable is of the moral kind, and appears no less elegant than easy to interpret. For pleasures proceed from plenty and affluence, attended with activity or exultation of the mind. Anciently their first incentives were quick, and seized upon men as if they had been winged, but learning and philosophy afterwards prevailing, had at least the power to lay the mind under some restraint, and make it consider the issue of things, and thus deprived pleasures of their wings.

This conquest redounded greatly to the honor and ornament of the Muses ; for after it appeared, by the example of a few, that philosophy could introduce a contempt of pleasures, it immediately seemed to be a sublime thing that could raise and elevate the soul, fixed in a manner down to the earth, and thus render men's thoughts, which reside in the head, winged as it were, or sublime.

Only the mother of the Sirens was not thus plumed on the head, which doubtless denotes superficial learning, invented and used for delight and levity ; an eminent example whereof we have in Petronius, who, after receiving sentence of death, still continued his gay frothy humor, and, as Tacitus observes, used his learning to solace or divert himself, and instead of such discourses as give firmness and constancy of mind, read nothing but loose poems and verses. Such learning as this seems to pluck the crowns again from the Muses' heads, and restore them to the Sirens.

The Sirens are said to inhabit certain islands, because pleasures generally seek retirement, and often shun society. And for their songs, with the manifold artifice and destructiveness thereof, this is too obvious and common to need explanation. But that particular of the bones stretching like white cliffs along the shores, and appearing afar off, contains a more subtile allegory, and denotes that the examples of others' calamity and misfortunes, though ever so manifest and apparent, have yet but little force to deter the corrupt nature of of man from pleasures.

This allegory of the remedies against the Sirens is not difficult, but very wise and noble : it proposes, in effect, three remedies, as well against subtile as violent mischiefs, two drawn from philosophy and one from religion.

The first means of escaping is to resist the earliest temptation in the beginning, and diligently avoid and cut off all occasions that may solicit or sway the mind ; and this is well represented by shutting up the ears, a kind of remedy to be necessarily used with mean and vulgar minds, such as the retinue of Ulysses.

But noble spirits may converse, even in the midst of pleasures, if the mind be well guarded with constancy and resolution. And thus some delight to make a severe trial of their own virtue, and thoroughly acquaint themselves with the folly and madness of pleasures, without complying or being wholly given up to them ; which is what Solomon professes of himself when he closes the account of all the numerous pleasures he gave a loose to, with this expression—" But wisdom still continued with me." Such heroes in virtue may, therefore, remain unmoved by the greatest incentives to pleasure, and stop themselves on the very precipice of danger ; if, according to the example of Ulysses, they turn a deaf ear to pernicious counsel, and the flatteries of their friends and companions, which have the greatest power to shake and unsettle the mind.

But the most excellent remedy, in every temptation, is that of Orpheus, who, by loudly chanting and resounding the praises of the gods, confounded the voices, and kept himself from hearing the music of the Sirens ; for divine contemplations exceed the pleasures of sense, not only in power but also in sweetness.

www.ingramcontent.com/pod-product-compliance
Lightning Source LLC
Chambersburg PA
CBHW031450270326
41930CB00007B/935